FINDING THE PATH

The search for spiritual reality

Roger Forster

f r a m e w o r k s

FRAMEWORKS
38 De Montfort Street, Leicester LE1 7GP, England

First published 1980 by Inter-Varsity Press under the title Saturday Night . . . Monday Morning.

British Library Cataloguing in Publication Data
Forster, Roger
Finding the path – New rev. ed.
1. Christian life
I. Title II. Forster, Roger. Saturday night – Monday morning
248.4
ISBN 0–85111–218–8

Set in 10 on 12pt Palatino
Typeset in Great Britain by Input Typesetting Ltd, London SW19 8DR
Printed in Great Britain by Cox & Wyman Ltd, Reading, Berkshire

Frameworks is an imprint of Inter-Varsity Press, the book-publishing division of the Universities and Colleges Christian Fellowship.

CONTENTS

INTRODUCTION

Finding the path is a search common to everyone. Whether it's expressed in pop and rock music or theatre and the visual arts, everyone is looking to find a higher plane, a truer love or a sense of meaning, purpose and identity, some direction in life. For some this quest has, more recently, turned to the East and the various gurus, mantras, astrologers and New Age experiences which are gaining increasing popularity, especially among the young.

This book joins in the search. It was born out of my attempts to communicate the relevant and reasonable Christian message in varied university situations, sharing with thinking people about life. I offer these pages in the hope that others might make the same discoveries as I have made in finding the path: in understanding what life is about; why we are here and where it all began.

Whatever are our impressions – perceptions concerning church, church history, religious wars or TV evangelists – nevertheless Jesus, who said he was the way, the truth and life, still appeals to genuine seekers. His love, simple lifestyle, courage, insights, denial for others, humility and genuine love of life caught my imagination when a student and still do today with increasing measure and persuasion.

Roger Forster

WHO NEEDS GOD?

CHAPTER 1

Let us suppose the universe has neither beginning nor end. Time stretches infinitely backwards and forwards. The whole system of time and space has no beginning; we have an *eternal universe*.

finding yourself

Now, if I want to know what it is all about and where my part is in it, then I have to find that meaning by looking into everything there is. Since there is nothing beyond the eternal universe, I stand here and I look into time and space, and I try to understand: Is

"Is there a voice? Is there a god?"

"Where did it all come from?"

anything coming to me? Is there a voice? Is there a god? Is there a world . . . a soul . . . something that speaks back? Or is there some totality of which I am a part which registers in my being and says, 'This is it!'? Can I find some unifying principle in a universe?

Some people think *happiness* is the only meaning of existence. But then Count Sade was happy in cruelty and gave his name to sadism. So how can happiness be the sole principle that determines every action? One person's happiness may cause another's misery.

Others say, 'I see some *inevitable dialectic* at work.' So Hegel, followed by Marx, claimed.

Others have found an evolving principle. And so the suggestions go on.

The sombre opinion of most twentieth-century thinkers, however, is that there is absolutely nothing there, nothing at all. Empty, meaningless!

All you can do is to make your own choice and live for that for as long as you wish or are able. There is no meaning to existence.

But, of course, there is another possibility.

Something or nothing?

If the universe has not always existed, then it must have had a beginning. This is the only other answer to the question, 'Where did it all come from?' This seems to fit in much better with our present scientific knowledge and it is perfectly legitimate to suggest that the universe began at a certain point.

But how did it begin? Did *some*-thing – this vast universe – come out of *no*-thing? We make such distinctions between something and nothing, somebody and nobody; surely something could not have come out of nothing.

So, if there was a beginning, there must have been a Beginner in some form or other: *Something* that existed eternally. Not an eternal universe this time, but an eternal *God*, who made time and space. This is where the Bible begins: 'In the beginning God' – an eternal God outside of time – 'created the heavens and the earth' – made space, energy and matter. That presupposition is equally, if not more, reasonable than our first one.

But it also brings in another avenue of investigation if I am to discover why I am here and for what I was made. Because I don't only have the universe to investigate, but I also have the one who began it.

Let us put it this way. Imagine you are going around a scientific laboratory and you ask an enthusiastic devotee of science (who is not quite over his sixth-form omniscience) to show you round. Then you find in one corner an old battered kettle, boiling away over a bunsen burner. You ask, '*Why* is this kettle boiling?' 'Oh, it's perfectly simple: gas is mixing with air, combustion is taking place, because energy goes into the water in the form of heat, making a vapour of greater volume than the water.' 'Yes,' you say, 'but *why* is the kettle boiling?' And he says, 'This *is* why it is boiling.'

"Can you please tell me why?"

Despairingly you turn to the lab assistant who runs the place and you ask, 'Can you please tell me why this kettle is boiling?' 'Of course, mate, I want a cup of tea'.

The first answer is perfectly legitimate as

we look into time and space with its cause-effect reactions. They explain the 'why?' of how. But for the 'why?' of *purpose*, we have to go to the person who put the kettle on in the first place. And if someone did set the universe in motion, if there is an eternal God, then it makes sense to ask him what it is all about.

finding freedom

". . . it makes sense to ask him . . ."

'Of course,' someone might say, 'finding God and asking him about our meaning and purpose might not be such a good idea.' After all this God figure (for we have still to define 'him', 'her' or 'it') may want to impose restrictions on us and limit our freedom. It is a risky business if we want to live our own lives and do as we please.

Freedom. From as far back as the second millennium BC, when Moses led a liberation march out of Egypt, to the overthrow of communist dictatorships in Eastern Europe in our own day, freedom has been the age-old quest. The frustrated tears of childhood, the aggression of the adolescent, the frequent defiance of authority: all these are strivings after freedom. The very word calls forth a response deep in our being.

Jesus well understood this longing of the human heart. Like all good revolutionary leaders he offered his followers freedom, but first he had something to say about what freedom is and what it is not. He did this in very homely terms, so that no-one could fail to grasp his point. He told a story:

A man had two sons. When the younger told his father, 'I want my share of your estate now, instead of waiting until you die,' his father agreed to divide his wealth between his sons.

A few days later this younger son packed all his belongings and took a trip to a distant land, and there wasted all his money on parties and prostitutes. About the time his money was gone a great famine swept over the land, and he began to starve. He persuaded a local farmer to hire him to feed his pigs. The boy became so hungry that even the pods he was feeding the swine looked good to him. And no one gave him anything.

When he finally came to his senses, he said to himself, 'At home even the hired men have enough and to spare, and here I am, dying of hunger! I will go home to my father and say, "Father, I have sinned against both heaven and you, and am no longer worthy of being called your son. Please take me on as a hired man." '

So he returned home to his father. And while he was still a long distance away, his father saw him coming, and was filled with loving pity and ran and embraced him and kissed him.

His son said to him, 'Father, I have sinned against heaven and you, and am not worthy of being called your son –'

But his father said to the slaves, 'Quick! Bring the finest robe in the house and put it on him. And a jewelled ring for his finger, and shoes! And kill the calf we have in the fattening pen. We must celebrate with a feast. For this son of mine was dead and has returned to life. He was lost and is found.' So the party began.

(Luke 15:11–24, Living Bible)

In this story Jesus came straight to our basic problem, which is that, in our attempts to find freedom, we have severed the essential link that a creature has with the Creator. The young man virtually says, 'Father, I wish you were dead.' (You don't usually get an inheritance until the person is dead, do you?)

"Father, I wish you were dead."

Jesus is highlighting the problem of the whole human race: we want to be rid of a Father God, to break out of all the God-talk which lies over our society, all these restrictions of 'this is right and that is wrong'; We want to be free! As in the story, we feel we have a right to our own life without the restrictions of a father, however loving. Consciously or unconsciously, we want God out.

It is no modern phenomenon to wish God dead or indeed to be an atheist. One thousand years before Jesus Christ, King David wrote about those who say 'there is no god'. In the sixth century BC the Chavakas of India were atheists. Buddhism too, in its classical form, is fundamentally atheistic. Then Jesus came, claiming to be God's extension into the world, the Son of God, God communicating with humanity. It was inevitable that he should come to a violent end. If it were not a crucifixion it would be an electric chair, or something similar. We do not want God interfering too much in his society. Along with the Son we want him dead.

Is God dead?

"We want to be free!"

Perhaps we thought that as adults with great ability, strength and prowess, it was at last time, as another expressed it, to roll the God-boulder right off the human scene and pitch it over the precipice and into the abyss. But we had forgotten that we are tied to that boulder and the rope is not limitless but fast running out. Suddenly a yank comes on that rope and we too pitch over the precipice. It is not just God who is dead, but us also. There is no destiny for the human race which has pitched its Creator over the edge. We die with our God.

It is exactly this picture that Jesus put before us in the story. When at the end the boy returns, his father says, 'My son was dead, but he is alive again; he was lost, but is now found.' For it is when we can solve this problem of the deadness of God to us that we discover that we have come alive again too. It is only when we put God back in his place, at the foundation of all things, that we discover that men and women can be something after all.

"We die with our God."

Not that the onus is entirely on us. This 'God' that we might try to repress is continually seeking to re-surface in our consciousness, taking us by surprise when we least expect it. In the first century when Jesus came as God's revelation, and was crucified accordingly, it was inevitable, if he were indeed the eternal God, that somehow or other his grave should burst open and men and women should discover that Jesus was alive again. For God is involved with the human race; that's why he became a person, wrapped up in our very cells and chemicals. His heart beat into the human scene and moved into our affairs with compassion and love: talking, working, laughing, crying, dying – yes, the God who entered into our very dying! It is the same resurrection God who keeps disturbing us now and says 'Look, I'm still here! How about coming home?'

finding answers

Jesus pierces our indifference and penetrates our hearts with his story of the lost son. He gets to the root of our problem and shows that individually we do matter. It is not just a sociological or political answer, though of course Christianity has implications there; nor is it just a philosophical answer. Rather it is a personal answer. The human race is made up of individuals. If each of them counts for nothing, then the whole of humanity counts for nothing, for 5,000 million times nothing still equals nothing.

". . . 5,000 million times nothing still equals nothing."

This is why Jesus made his message a personal one, put in terms of personal relationships in a story. Like the son, we have rejected the origin of our being, cut ourselves loose from the source of our life, and are dying in our attempts to 'go it alone'. If this personal disease cannot be stemmed, then the epidemic of today's world-wide problems will never be solved. For the recovery begins with each of us finding the answer with Christ, allowing his healing to take place in our own experience. We will contribute to the world's well-being only when we have got the problem put straight in ourselves.

the face

So the boy cuts loose. He quickly glances round to see if he is cutting a good figure. But unfortunately he only catches a glimpse of his father's face, pain written on it, saying nothing. Love cannot coerce.

In the far country where the son seeks his

emancipation, there is free, riotous living with no guidelines, no absolutes, just pleasing oneself. He may have had momentary twinges of reason: 'How can you be sure you are being yourself if you don't know what you are meant to be?' And he must have had times when he threw himself on his bed in disgust or dissatisfaction after some new experience which he had hoped would liberate him. He dreams fitfully of the face of his father, a distant memory repressed.

". . . the ache that occurs . . ."

In the unconscious of everyone there lies the image of our Father's face. The face behind the universe, which now and then emerges, seeking to surface into our very consciousness. Nietzsche called it 'sea-sickness', Sartre 'Nausea'. Perhaps it is more 'homesickness'. It is the ache that occurs when we are alone on a mountain; or when the sun sets and we want to worship and don't know what to worship; or when we wish that some innocent childhood experience would return. We ache and we are sick, and we know there is a face behind the universe trying to get through again – you know the moments. Times when we have been confronted with our own real sickness.

We can try to escape by abandoning ourselves to some new sex experience, some lust after power, perhaps the greed for money, experimentation in drugs, violence, the occult. But we are not really free at all.

". . . when the sun sets . . ."

Nevertheless we still press on. Even though there's not even a glimmer coming through to assure us that there is something at the end of the road. So then, inevitably there is that terrible business of having to go on play-acting. We don't know who we are;

we don't know what we are meant to be; we are like beings who are lost in a vast world, not sure of anything.

". . . the punch-line . . ."

the homecoming

Sadly, we rarely take account of our ultimate meaning or of God until we are lonely and hungry. The central figure of Jesus' story was so hungry he would have eaten the pigs' food. After all, if he was just a clump of chemicals, a materialistic beast, he might as well live like an animal.

Somehow, though, that answer didn't seem to solve the problem. There is more to us than just animal responses. So his hunger grew. Now Jesus comes to the punch-line, perhaps the most profound point of the whole parable:

'And when he came to himself . . .' – when he discovered who he was – 'he said *"Father* . . . I will go to my *father"*.' When he breathed out that one simple word 'father' he realized his identity. For it is when men and women dare to open their mouths and say 'Father' that they make the most profound discovery of their being.

When we start to call God 'Father', we are touching something which is most fundamental and deep. We were meant to bear his character, share his life, have rapport with his wisdom, enter into his mind and heart, taste his love.

"Now that is *difficult."*

This is true Christianity. This is true humanity. This is the path. We were meant to have that fulfilment of our own personality as it encounters and involves itself with the

Person who lies behind this universe.

But it is not so much the 'father' part of the son's confession which we find difficult as the 'I have sinned.' Now that *is* difficult. It is a confession of need, of wrong; it is an acknowledgment that I have not come up to what I intended for myself, let alone the purpose for which I was made: for God. Such failure is entirely my responsibility.

This realization needn't be an emotional thing; it is bare factual acknowledgment that I have not lived in relationship with him. It is what the Bible in other places calls 'repentance', changing our mind about God and about ourselves, and telling him so. 'I will go to my father, and I will say to him, "Father, I have sinned . . .".'

Jesus tells that the father eagerly comes running down the road to welcome his son – 'Father, I have sinned . . . and am not worthy of being called your son . . .', and before he could get any more words out the father interrupts him, 'Quick! Bring the finest robe . . .' God has come running out to us just where we are, in Jesus. And on the cross God is welcoming us back with a reconciling kiss.

". . . a reconciling kiss."

C. S. Lewis was a lecturer at Oxford University when one day and for the first time he gave in and 'admitted that God was God'. At that moment he stepped out of atheism into an experience which he later described by the title of his book *Surprised by Joy*. 'I was the most reluctant convert in the whole of the British Isles,' he said. But when he was reconciled to God, he experienced to his surprise the 'feasting, music and dancing' of Christianity; he was surprised by joy.

C. S. Lewis, Surprised by Joy *(Fontana, 1959)*

His experience can be ours too: it is good to be home again, it is good to be alive!

touching the infinite

". . . where is this God?"

Just a minute, where is this God? We can't see him. They say he is everywhere. Even that sounds suspicious – perhaps he is nowhere! Who on earth *is* God anyway?

The question 'Show me your god' is a real one. Perhaps if there's a God he can never be touched or known; and those moments of ache and longing in our hearts, those moments of shame when we feel we want forgiveness, those times when we look around saying, 'Is there some meaning or some purpose?', perhaps they are all just mere mockings of our own hearts: that we can seek but never find.

But that would be as bad as creating us with a hunger for food and yet not providing us with the means to eat. Is God like that? And, anyway, who would want to meet him? If he's so inhuman he deserves to be locked up!

If there is a God who can be known at all on earth, he is one who somehow comes through from the infinite into the space-time situation in which we live, and communicates at our level. The 'coming through' of God we could compare with the music of a magnificent orchestral piece being reduced to a piano piece: although the piano plays exactly the same melody as the whole orchestra, the depth, the profundity and the diversity can only be brought out by the hundred and one different instruments. In one sense something is lost, but nevertheless the whole tune is there.

Christians claim something of this order has happened between the infinite and the finite. Jesus Christ, as the piano setting of the music of the infinite God, can say, '. . . the Father is greater than I', but can add, 'Anyone who has seen me has seen the Father.' So St Paul asserts concerning Jesus: 'For in Christ all the fulness of the Deity lives in bodily form.'

(John 14:28; 14:9)

(Colossians 2:9)

Coming through

The claims of Jesus to deity are not unreasonable claims at all. If God is going to communicate with us, how otherwise could he adequately have done it, but by becoming human? God could speak to us through the very structure, logic and pattern of the universe. There is a certain amount of information one could glean from space and time, though it does not appear to say too much. Or maybe God could speak to us through the very beauty that exists, but there is a certain amount of ugliness too, and it leaves us perplexed. Or perhaps he could speak to us through our consciences, because he has given us the ability to say: This is wrong and that is right – especially when we view others' actions or political stances. But, unfortunately conscience, so often, can be determined by environment.

". . . just mere mockings of our own hearts . . ."

God could become a great mountain or tree or something. But that would only say he is big or that he blows in the breeze. Maybe he could become an animal and snuggle up against my knee? Well, that would only tell me he is rather snugly and warm.

Of course, there is only one door open: if God is going to communicate so that we can know something of why he made this universe, he can only do so on our particular wave-length. He has to become a *human*. And the reasonableness of it all is evident in that we didn't even have to open a Bible to discover it; we could have just sat down and thought, and it might have come through. Ultimately God would have to have a heart, hands, brain – a body that enters into the very scenes we are in and, therefore, speaks our human language.

". . . the reasonableness of it all is evident . . ."

If we accept this, how would he go about it? Such a profoundly important revelation would require careful preparation. Maybe he would start with someone like Abraham, with whom God could communicate by means of dreams and visions, and even more deeply, inwardly, through his spirit and conscience. From his family, God could build up a whole race and continue to reveal more and more of his ultimate purpose. When God did finally make himself fully known in the person of Jesus, there would be a nation able to comprehend what it was all about and who Jesus was. Israel was that nation. Thus God prepared the environment of his revelation for centuries beforehand.

Now when at last he came into this world, would he enter by the normal process of birth? A human would need to have a normal birth and foetal experience. Yet inevitably there would be something unusual about the way he came in. Perhaps a virgin conception is not so strange if he is both God and human.

And we would not be surprised, would we, if this 'God as a person' did a miracle or two. For, after all, it would not be a very full revelation of God if he did not show his creative power. We would also expect him to do a bit of teaching of ethics. Not really 'way-out' stuff, because it is only cranks who introduce new ethics; it would be the sort of teaching which, by and large, we realize is the right sort of way we should live (although his theological teaching might be a little unusual!).

However, as we have seen, if he really were God, we could not let him go through the whole span of life without rejecting him. We should have to throw him out, and do it rather violently.

But if this revelation of God died, we would not expect him to remain dead, would we? It would be another matter if he were only human. We wouldn't expect a repeat: we live and die once. But he is not dismissed so easily.

Of course, we can overlook him and ignore him and pretend he was not there, and never would be there. But the unfortunate thing is that the harder we try to run away, the faster God seems to interrupt us with his resurrection-Jesus; he keeps cropping up when we thought we had got rid of him.

C. S. Lewis writes: 'The discrepancy between the depth, sincerity, and may I say the shrewdness of His moral teaching, unless He is indeed God, have never been got over. . . We cannot patronisingly look at the teaching of Jesus Christ, and say, Yes, He was a good man and quite a good teacher, for

He did not leave us with that alternative. He is either on the level of a man who thinks he is a poached egg, a raving lunatic, or he is an arch-demon deliberately deceiving mankind, OR, as He claims to be, he is God.' Mad, bad . . . or God? Lunatic, liar, . . . or Lord? The person of Jesus Christ demands a verdict.

C. S. Lewis, Mere Christianity *(Fontana, 1970), p. 52*

twist in the tail

Of course, this creates a problem for us today. If those of the first century in Galilee and Judea could see Jesus, hear him and understand his birth, life, teaching, death and resurrection, what about us today?

Perhaps that is where the most startling part of the story takes place, and that, perhaps, we would not have guessed. For God offers to take the Spirit of that *person* (which he was) and put that Spirit, that light source, that life power, that motivating drive, into each of our lives. He calls that his own life, eternal life, because it belongs to the eternal God, or the *Jesus* life, the life we saw in Jesus. And that life, living in his people, to a greater or lesser extent, goes on saying something like the same things, and tries to live out the same sort of life and bring the same sort of communication. Christ, we say, lives *in* the believer.

". . . the most startling part of the story . . ."

LOVE IS. . .

When Jesus told the story about the Good Samaritan (the one where a beaten-up man is twice ignored by religious people who 'pass him by on the other side') he was teaching about costly love. Eventually the hero turns out to be a Samaritan who helps the man to shelter and promises to pay for his care. This is someone who is about as unlikely to help a Jew in distress as a devout Arab would be today. Jesus is being typically controversial. This is no wet wimp talking – Jesus was risking his life.

Costly love is at the heart of real Christianity. Jesus' anecdote teaches that being like the religious people and having the right answers or even living a devout religious life, helps no-one. It's living out love, costly love, that counts.

Some years ago a Korean Christian pastor learned that his two sons had died in a college political riot. When order had been restored and the murderers brought to court, the bereaved father pleaded for these men, offering his home in which they could finish their education while on probation. One young man refused, but the other accepted and the pastor received and loved him in the place of his own boys. Today that murderer is himself a preacher of Christ's message.

'Where does such love come from?' we might ask, as surely as Jesus turned to the audience of his Good Samaritan story (one lawyer to be precise) and said 'go and do likewise'. We may be challenged and attracted by this kind of dangerous, universal, excessive and non-calculating love, but how can we find the power to live it out? And what right has Jesus to call us to this anyway?

It is these questions to which we now turn. For the Good Samaritan, like the Korean pastor, is reflecting the life and love of Jesus. A life in which Jesus loved to death.

"What right has Jesus . . ."

TO HELL WITH GOD

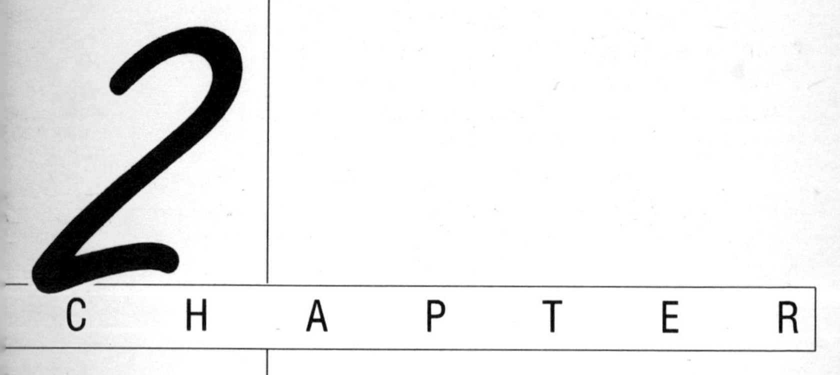

C H A P T E R

" . . . attractive, vital, gifted . . ."

Death – anyone's death – raises in most thinking people the question 'Why?' The younger the person, the more attractive, vital, gifted, promising they were, the more insistently that question hammers into our brains, '*Why*? What is the point of it? What waste! What a senseless negation of everything good! Why did it have to be?'

When Jesus died in the prime of life, at the height (seemingly) of his powers and popularity, having brought such hope to so many, the same questions slammed into the consciousness of his followers and almost shattered them. Yet Jesus himself had taught them that his death was not only inevitable, it was essential. He was born to die. His disciples came to understand, and then to preach with such power, that the crucifixion of Jesus Christ was the fundamental root of his message.

(Matthew 16:21)

The cross has become a world-wide symbol for Christianity. Christ called his followers to take up their crosses and follow him. Paul said that he gloried in the cross of Christ. Remembering that the cross was the Roman Empire's foulest and cruellest gibbet – only fit for slaves – isn't it a sick mind that can take delight in such a torturous death? The stench and blood and agony of such an execution can surely only excite the morbid interest of a perverted, dehumanized individual.

(Galatians 6:14)

Truly there is something very offensive in Christ's message of crucifixion. A modern writer speaks of it as the 'gospel of gore' and suggests that we emphasize the beauty of Christ's life and teaching while passing over this repugnant article of faith. There is something in us that responds to such a suggestion. After all, true religion should emphasize the beautiful and living, and try to eradicate the dark and seamy side of truth. Thus many have tried to revamp the message of Jesus and remove that which is offensive to sensitive, sophisticated and squeamish twentieth-century minds.

". . . Jesus died in the prime of life . . ."

the seamy side of life

The problem of such a renovated, updated

message is that there seems to be very little of Christianity left. After all, a third of the gospel material (Matthew, Mark, Luke and John) is centred on the event of the crucifixion or the preparation for it. Jesus said he had come to give his life as a ransom for many. The whole gospel material flows toward this point. This is not because the first century in which it was written was less mature or sophisticated than ours, and consequently found the death of Jesus a less offensive subject.

(Mark 10:45)

On the contrary, a graffito of the early church period has been found depicting someone worshipping the head of an ass on a cross, with the inscription 'Alexamenos worships his god' – a cruel jibe by his fellows at a Christian's obnoxious faith. It seems it was no easier for an early believer than it is for one today to cross this initial grotesque and psychologically offensive barrier when trying to communicate his faith to others.

". . . a Christian's obnoxious faith."

Had you gone to the intelligentsia of the day who boasted their Greek culture, you would not have found an easy acceptance there either. To go to those who delighted in the refined excellence of the body, mind and aesthetic aspirations – who said that in the perfection of mind and body we have the answer to the world's needs – to present to them Christ crucified as an object of worship was asking for outright repudiation. The Greek culture could never be expected to accept that the answer to the predicament of men and women was a crucified criminal, Jesus Christ. They would have stumbled (as Paul said), been offended at the offence, the stumbling-block of the cross. For Calvary

(1 Corinthians 1:18–23)

spells death to the pride that presumes that we in our majesty and development and maturity can solve the predicament of the human race. It declares that we need a blood sacrifice in order to find an answer to the problems of the world, and that was abhorrent to the cultured Greek.

". . . offended at the offence of the cross."

Even if you went to the most religious people of the day, the Jews, with their genius for religion, and declared to them that God's answer to people's needs was the Lamb of God that bore away the sin of the world on the cross of Calvary, you would inevitably have faced objections and distaste, for it was in the Hebrew sacred writings that someone who was hung on a tree was evidently cursed of God. How could you expect a Jewish religionist to be moved by a message that said: God himself has spoken to the world through the blood of Jesus, through the death of one who was hung on a tree?

(Galatians 3:13, quoting Deuteronomy 21:23)

All in bad taste. In the first century the message of the cross invited the hostility of the governing power, the intelligentsia, and the religious leaders. Yet Christians were so fired by the magnetism of the cross of Christ that they could not stop talking about it. They told of Christ dying at Calvary crying, 'My God, my God, why have you forsaken me?' In that cry of dereliction and desolation, they said, God is answering the cry of the world and meeting the dead situation of humanity. They were fired with the love which the blood of the cross seemed to spill out into their experience. There was something about it that made them, every time they began to talk about Jesus, very soon

(Matthew 27:46)

"My God, my God, why have you forsaken me?"

add, '. . . and he was crucified, but God has raised him up'. It was the fundamental issue, and still is today, of the true Christian message – *Christ died*.

". . . the most significant death of history."

Despite its apparent distastefulness and lack of sophistication, despite the suggested unhealthiness of people being taken up all the time with death and blood – despite all that – the event of Jesus' dying has been a magnetic point for men and women through century after century, especially to those who have desired to understand the meaning of life and death. Even Rousseau, no friend of Christianity, compared the death of Jesus with that of Socrates, for Socrates died as a wise man: taking the cup of hemlock from his executioner who was weeping, he blessed him, and turning to his friends he sought to comfort them. His was the death of a sage.

But the death of Jesus as he hung on the cross midst hatred and shame and spitting, as he cried out in desolation saying, 'Father, forgive them; for they know not what they do', 'that', says Rousseau, 'is *the death of a god*', something superhuman, something that takes you by surprise. Muggeridge calls it the most significant death of history. The great nineteenth-century preacher, Charles Spurgeon, died saying 'My theology becomes very simple – Jesus died for me.' Even Christians who understand very little about their faith know the fundamental truth grasped by their own spirits that makes meaning and sense out of everything that they are experiencing in their Christian walk. Yes, Jesus died for me. There is something about the death of Jesus Christ which is compelling and commanding. It makes us look, even if we

Vernon C. Grounds, The Reason for our Hope, *pp. 34–35*

don't want to. 'And when I am lifted up,' says Christ, referring to his execution, 'I will draw everyone to me.' We have to take it into account. What does it mean?

(John 12:32–33)

Getting involved

One meaning is clear enough. Jesus died for sinners, we say. Well, he really did! He loved the harlots, the quislings, the tax-collectors and the ordinary people who were not counted for much and certainly were not religious. It was because Jesus *did* love those sorts of people that eventually he had to die. He died because he was concerned about the prostitutes, whom all decent people resented because of their threat to stable families and their resultant luxurious living. He died because he loved selfish traitors who made themselves rich by taxing the ordinary people on behalf of the foreign occupation. Any liberationist, moralist, religionist or socially conscious reformer could see Jesus was only fit to die. He died because he *would* love rejected people who knew that they needed help, love, reintegration, and above all, God. He died for those who themselves knew, and everyone else knew, were sinners.

They listened to what he had to say and wanted to share the health and the love that he was pouring out to men and women from his own presence; they wanted to know God, or copy somehow or other the way that he seemed to walk with dignity; they wanted to live on this earth in the right way – even though they hadn't before. Those are the people for whom Jesus died. In fact, in a

". . . eventually he had to die."

sense he died for all of us with any need – and that is everyone, if only we understand ourselves aright.

". . . he could open up a gate in our very death . . ."

Sometimes the New Testament writers struggled with the Old Testament pictures of sacrifice. Sometimes they used first-century legal terms, like 'to justify' or to make right: Christ died to make us right with God. Sometimes they used the word 'propitiation' which has to do with exhausting wrath, so that God's reaction to man's sin can be in some way or other worked out and exhausted in order that we might come into the peace of his heart. Just as light always reacts to darkness to destroy it, God always reacts to sin to destroy that.

But somehow God has found a way in the death of Jesus whereby his reaction fell there and he is able to welcome enemies as friends. It is evident that the New Testament writers are being stretched, with the help of God's Spirit, to explain and to get to the depths of this terrific event.

Getting personal

". . . two things come through loud and clear."

Yet there is still a mystery in the cross. That is not surprising because what was happening on the cross was not something which arose out of people's ingenuity or speculation, nor an invention of the human brain. On the contrary, it was something which was born out of the mind and heart of God. It was God who devised the plan to get involved with us, to get involved with our death, so that somehow or other he could open up a gate in our very death and declare life through himself.

It is impossible finally to plumb the total meaning of the mystery of Christ crucified, but we may still benefit from it. The nourishment of a good meal can be experienced and profited from without a total grasp of the nutritious value in terms of calories, carbohydrates, proteins and vitamins.

Nonetheless, two things come through loud and clear. One is that the crucifixion of Jesus Christ, although making available something for everyone, must be participated in *personally*. Paul puts it like this: 'The son of God, who loved me and gave himself for *me*'; or John can write: 'God so loved the world that he gave his only Son, that *whoever* believes . . .', and again, '. . . So the Son of man must be lifted up (to die), that *everyone* believes in him . . .' 'Everyone' – this is the individual personal response that is necessary to this event of the cross. For if Christ prays, 'Father, forgive . . .' there is the need that I personally should come and drink the sweetness of that forgiveness and make it mine.

(Galatians 2:20)

(John 3:14–16)

(Luke 23:24)

Then I can begin to say: The Son of God loved *me* and gave himself for *me*. As an individual I start to be involved in the effects of Christ's crucifixion. Calvary must be personally appropriated, so that I can say with Paul, it was 'for me'.

Secondly, what comes through loud and clear is that Christ's crucifixion has something fundamentally to do with *sin*. Sin dehumanizes our humanness, for it is a breakaway from the definition that God has given us. We step outside the boundary of our definition when we resent, when we are bitter, unloving, brutal, base or lustful, and our true human nature is destroyed. That is sin: disobedience to the God-appointed definition of what it means to be a human being. This definition is perfectly measured out in the humanity of Jesus; coming short of that beauty in our lives is sin, and it is in the realm of sin that we must understand Jesus' death. Paul says 'the wages of sin is death'. Christ died because of sin – not his, but ours.

(Romans 6:23)

Moral blackmail

There are those who object to the Christian message of Christ dying for the world by saying that it is a kind of moral blackmail. Christ died – well, it forces you to make some sort of response to him, out of sympathy, out of sheer decency.

"Now just watch!"

There is a sense in which that is true. When I became a Christian, it was primarily seeing Christ dying that moved me to some responsive action. I felt, 'Well, I must do something about it.' So it is sometimes charged that this is moral blackmail, as though God did something (if it is true that he did) which forces us to respond out of sheer humanity. If he went to such lengths to show me his love, we might say, then I had better respond.

Now that would be blackmail if it were not that God was also doing something necessary *for us* when Jesus died. Let us put it like this: Suppose you were going for a walk with your girl friend, along the side of a fast-flowing river. You are no swimmer. You say to your girl friend, 'I love you so much, I would die for you. Now just watch!' And you dive into the stream and sail down the torrent. The last she sees of you are the bubbles that arise in the distance! You could say, 'Well, there you are, that just shows how much I love you' (but you wouldn't say it because you would not be there to say it!). However, I don't think she would be particularly impressed. She would probably say, 'Well, it's a good thing he did not become my husband and the father of my children, because he would have been thoroughly irresponsible!' I don't think she would be too impressed by the quality of your love.

In the death of Christ, God is not just showing how much he loves us – at least, not that alone, although that is true. Let us rather put it like this: suppose the girl falls into the river and her lover then pitches himself into the torrent; he can't swim, but he just manages to push her to the bank, and with his last push falls back himself. Once again the bubbles rise to give evidence that this lover died for the loved one. Now the girl, for the rest of her life, would say, 'Yes, he really did love me.' Whatever happened to her afterwards, no matter whom she gives herself to, she would say, 'That man really loved me. He gave his life to save mine.' What Jesus is doing at Calvary is not just making a great demonstration; he is dying the world's death; he is getting into the predicament that we are in, in order to extricate us. That is why we declare that in the death of Christ we see the depth and the height and the breadth, indeed, the whole measurement of the love of God. He did something about our predicament that is going to save us.

"He gave his life to save mine."

". . . dying the world's death . . ."

DON'T TALK ABOUT SIN

3

C H A P T E R

There are those who say that they don't like all this blood talk, all the 'gospel of gore' stuff. After all, it is a little horrific – why major on the suffering side? Why not just talk about the other?

". . . the world is hellish to millions of people . . ."

But let us ask ourselves, Do we really think that God has anything to say to this sort of world, with all its violence, its bloodshed, its bitterness, privations and oppression, that does not have to be spelt out ultimately in all the bloodiness of the cross? In a bloody world we need a violent message; and the violence of Calvary is God speaking to men and women who need to know that in this world there is a God who has met that violence and taken the blow on his own heart. If God had not spoken to us in the stark terms of blood, then we twentieth-century products with all our ability to destroy and to hate would never listen. The human blood that has wastefully flowed in rivers down the centuries would have nothing to answer it from an almighty God, unless he speaks in that *milieu*. We might invent some vague idealistic song, but that would be no realistic message for dying and violent men.

". . . they were dying like flies."

It is in the blood of the cross that God is speaking to our hellish world. Don't forget that it *is* hellish to millions of people who do not sit as we do in the ease of Western culture (although that also is fast eroding and dying). For the majority of the world, life has been a suffering and sad tale, and God has spoken to the world in the cross of Jesus Christ in a way that begins to make sense in such a scene.

Love in action

E. Gordon, Miracle on the River Kwai *(Fontana, 1965)*

Some may have read Ernest Gordon's book *Miracle on the River Kwai* or will have seen the film *Bridge over the River Kwai*. They both relate the same time and event in the history of the last war, when prisoners of war were used in Burma to build in one year a railway which should have taken six years. They were beaten to work on this crash job; consequently they were dying like flies. Their conditions were hellish. There was no time to think about anybody but self if you were going to stay alive in that concentration

". . . he cocked his rifle and looked down the sights."

camp. Day after day men saw their friends turn against them, betraying them to the guards, stealing the few things they had left, just for the sheer . . . 'Well, I had better look after Jack because nobody else will!' It was a terrible situation, but one or two unusual things began to happen in that camp.

A few Christian men lived in a way that made people talk. There was a Scot, for instance, who regularly took his food down to his mate who was dying in the sick quarters (men in the sick quarters were not fed because they were not able to work). One day Jock died, debilitated with malnutrition. They had told Jock he was a fool to keep giving his food to a dying man. But his friend lived; Jock did not. It made people talk.

There was a time when a platoon was thought to have lost a tool. They were all marched out and the guard shouted and screamed that every one of them would die unless that tool was given back. Nobody moved. He shouted again that every one would die; he cocked his rifle and looked down the sights. One man took two paces forward, implying 'I took the tool'. The club of the rifle came down on his head and he was beaten mercilessly to death.

The platoon was marched back into the camp to the tool-shed. The missing tool was hanging in its place; it had never been missing. One man had given his life for his friends – something like Jesus did, on a mini-scale. Men asked, 'Who was this fellow?' He was a Christian.

In this situation, which was as near hell as it could get, the men went to an officer and asked, 'Do you have a Bible?' The officer said he had. They replied, 'We want to know if Christianity has anything to say to us in this scene.' The officer said, 'Supposing we read it and find out that it hasn't?' The men answered, 'Then at least we will know.' So they read and studied the Bible every night.

". . . as near hell as it could get . . ."

A spiritual revival took place amongst the men. Many of them came out of that camp as Christians, including the author of the book *Miracle on the River Kwai*. In Christ's cross God has something pretty straight to say to a violent world. If he had not, there would be no message for us at all.

The writer of that book about the River Kwai miracle had formerly thought, like many, that Christians spoke in terms of an angry father sending a loving son to die, who somehow or other appeased the anger of the father, and thereby brought people to heaven. This seemed to him immoral.

But this, too, is a misleading caricature of the meaning of the cross of Christ. The Bible declares that God himself was in Christ, reconciling the world to himself. The event of the crucifixion was not something to induce an unwilling God to be favourable towards men by the action of a third party. It was God's action. What God was doing, he was doing in and through Jesus Christ. That death was something which God himself accomplished.

What then is God saying to us through the death of Christ?

"This seemed to him immoral."

What sin does to us

God points to the cross, that most horrific

of all executions and says: That is what the human race is. That is what sin does to us, spelt out in the symbol of our flesh and blood, but expressing the very torture and agony of our personal souls. That is the dehumanizing that sin brings to the human frame, shattering human personality and breaking the spirit as it cried in desolation, 'My God, my God, why have you forsaken me?' In the moments of his execution Christ cried that desolate cry, depicting the very hell that exists in the human soul, and which cannot be extricated by man's therapy – the hell of shame and guilt, of lust and pride, the hell that burns within us and will go on burning even when our bodies have been stripped from our person. Hell begins in the human frame; and Jesus experienced it on the cross. God points to Calvary and says: That is what sin does to men and women.

"Hell begins in the human frame . . ."

In one of Christ's stories, he tells of someone who died and went to hell. He speaks of the thirst which the person longs to be slaked. If we thirst now, we shall thirst for ever, unless God can somehow get into that hell and salvage us out of it.

(Luke 16:19–31)

Perhaps there have been moments already in your life when you have troubled to stop and ask yourself questions about love, when you have wanted to act altruistically and haven't been able to. Hell begins in the human soul, and God has gone to hell to get us out of it. That was what he was doing on the cross.

The writer Sartre (who was, of course, an atheist) tells us his definition of hell: Three people find themselves sitting in a cell. They can't get out, there is a bright light and they

Jean-Paul Sartre, No Exit

are condemned to eternal sleeplessness. So they begin to chat with one another. It all starts quite nicely at first, but as they go on chatting they begin hurting one another. Suddenly, one of them realizes: 'This is a kind of economy in devil-power.' She says, 'We are in hell but each of us will act as torturer of the others.' The others scream and shout, demonstrating that she is correct, while trying to tell her that she is not. Here is Sartre's definition of hell – that though we are confined close together, our personalities are miles apart and never make contact.

The terrible, tragic loneliness of the twentieth century is but the overspill of hell. We were meant to be sons of God, knowing his life, sharing his wisdom, entering into his business, knowing him in the family of his love. Hell is the destruction of all that. 'My God, my God, why have you forsaken me?'

What sin does to God

If the crucifixion shows what sin does to us, it also shows us what sin does to God. For it is God who, in Jesus Christ, is entering into this human predicament. It is God who is taking this blow upon his being. Sin is doing something to God.

I remember some years ago seeing my son being hit by a truck on a road in Eastern Europe. I was unable to do a thing as the vehicle applied its brakes and my boy hesitated slightly, till the wing hit his head, throwing him into the air. I would have given everything to have stood over him or in his place. My father heart was stretched in the agony of those few seconds into what seemed an eternity as the inevitable impact took place. The pain of the blow reverberated in my own psychology – virtually as a physical impact.

Thank God, my son lived. Perhaps the blow I experienced helped me to understand in a small way the bruising God sustains in seeing the result of our sin. It hurts, and it hurt God.

When I begin to see that my living in God's world *my* way rather than God's way, hurts him, that is often the moment when I begin to say at last: I must do something about it. I must stop and begin to go God's way. It is the broken heart of God that is displayed as Jesus dies – for sin hurts the God of love who made us to be his children.

What God has done about that sin

If the crucifixion shows us what sin does to us and what sin does to God, it also shows us what God has done about that sin. In the Old Testament days, when people came to offer a sacrifice, there was audience participation. The worshipper would lay hands on the sacrifice and confess his sins over the animal, and then the animal would be slain. The sacrificer would go back home and continue in fellowship with God knowing that what was done to the sacrificial animal ought to be done to him. Something happened when Jesus died, which is *for* us and which we cannot do ourselves.

Think of a line of trucks on a railway track receiving an impact. One hits the first, and that one the next, and so on, till the impact bounces all the way down the line. So, in the closed circuit of this universe, sin with its repercussions bangs down from time forward and time backward to the very cross where God has come into time and space. Christ stands as a truck with the brake on, or as the buffers, to take the impact and to exhaust the effects of our sin.

If you saw the film *The Exorcist* (and I don't recommend it for those who didn't!) you will know what a horrific portrayal it is of the supernatural scene today. It is also an expression (though imperfect from a Christian perspective) of the only solution to the problem of evil. The psychiatrist takes the demonic force of the child upon himself, pitches himself through the window and dies, as a *substitute*, to save the child. For 2,000 years the Christian gospel has been declaring that, at Calvary, Jesus Christ is doing that to the power of evil and thereby removing the force of sin from people's lives so that we can become whole again.

"Something happened when Jesus died . . ."

Or let me put it another way. A woman and a man love one another and set up in marriage, having a home and children. Later, he goes off with another woman, perhaps two or three. Because she loves the man, the desertion hurts her, for she sees what he is doing to himself, as well as the mess he is making of other people's lives and hers. One day there is a bang at the door, and there is her husband standing outside.

He stands on one foot and then the other, not looking her in the eyes, more a mouse than a man. He says, 'I'm sorry, will you have me back?' Now, what is she going to

"Suddenly it snaps."

do? Will she reply nonchalantly, 'Oh yes, come in. There are your fish and chips, your favourite programme is on the telly, put your feet up!' Is that what she does? If you think so, I don't think you have ever been in love. It wouldn't be as cheap as that, not if you have really given yourself, as well as your body, and see people as people, not things. If you have loved, you know that. Rather, there would be a hesitation, a tension inside her.

Suddenly it snaps. Metaphorically she steps forward and stands in his shoes. She feels his condemnation, his self-judgment and fear. She feels all the consequences of his actions on herself. She puts out her arms – 'Of course I will' – there is a reconciling kiss; a new relationship has been formed. He need never have to fear now that she might reject him once she has discovered everything he has done and been, because she herself has experienced it all in its consequence, and knows what she has forgiven.

Now if you forgive someone something and it doesn't hurt, don't imagine you had anything to forgive. It has to hurt, otherwise there is nothing to forgive. That hurt is the evidence that you are beginning to appreciate what it has done to the other person. To some degree there is a rapport. Of course, in our human relationships, it may not be perfect, but to some degree there must be an empathy with that situation.

Once forgiven, never forsaken

What God is doing as Christ dies, amongst other things, is knowing what he is forgiving, that he might say, 'Of course I forgive you; come home.' He died that we might be forgiven, that we might know that we are forgiven, and that we might know that he will never annul our forgiveness and reject us. I know I am forgiven because Jesus died for me and I have accepted it. I know that God won't throw me out again because he knows what he has forgiven in Roger Forster. For he bore the consequences of all my sins, in fact, of everyone's sins, when Jesus hung on the cross.

Christ's death is the basis upon which we can know that we are accepted back into a relationship with God the Father, as his sons and daughters. We can begin to live with all the exuberance of the love of his presence, in the delight of his heart over his children's ways.

The cross of Jesus Christ still stands supreme in the final crisis of the soul – the crisis between God and us, the crisis between us and death, the crisis concerning sin, guilt and shame. The cross of Christ still stands supreme – in the crisis of evil, of spiritism and occultism, the powers that wreck the lives of men and women. We know that we have sinned, and the cross has got something to do with that. We personally need to come and say 'Thank you' to Christ for meeting us just where we are. There was nowhere else where he could meet us but in death, for we bear the marks of the death sentence which is written across our human race.

We know that inside we are dead, dead to God, dead to love, dead to other people. Jesus meets us just there. He says, 'I died for you.' Come and accept the forgiveness that he offers and the relationship with God which is what makes a person a Christian.

". . . the final crisis of the soul . . ."

DEAD END?

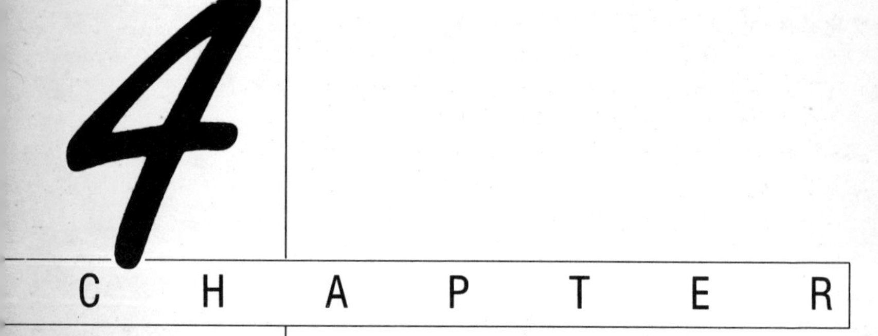

"Life is constituted of lust . . ."

You may have one of those modern up-dated Bibles. Some of us who are more used to the older version feel sorry that the modern versions are often not quite so beautiful, and have lost some of those beautiful nuances.

'Courage' is the name of a well-known beer in England

For instance, the passage where the apostle Paul is going to Rome as a prisoner, under guard, and he reaches a place just outside Rome, on the Appian Way; it is called 'Three Taverns'. There, the Authorized Version puts it, the Christian brothers came out to meet him, and they 'took courage . . .'. It is rather a shame when these poetic touches are lost in the newer versions!

As the apostle Paul proceeded along the Appian Way into Rome for his great trial before the Emperor, he would have passed the tombs of the great and mighty, which still stand there today, tombstones on which are carved the names of the rich, the political and militaristic leaders.

"... something to say worth hearing."

Carved on the tombs are little epitaphs which the incumbents have left to society; generally they are sarcastic. One of them, not too far down the road from the 'Three Taverns' perhaps, says: 'A cocktail for you and a cocktail for me. . . And that is life.' That is as much as he could be persuaded to pass on to posterity. You go on a little further, and there is another epitaph, a little more sophisticated; it says: 'Life is constituted of lust. But lust is not good for the constitution' – very profound and helpful, I am sure, for succeeding generations! Another is more sombre; it simply says: 'The sun will rise and set, but it is eternal darkness for . . .' (the person whose remains lie there). Now that is about as much as the great and mighty can say about this world and its life.

Interestingly enough, however, just a few years after Paul passed that way, many men and women who had discovered the reality of the message which Paul proclaimed throughout the world began to be buried in the catacombs, while hiding from persecution. Not all of the graves, of course, have been opened. But those that have, have something to say worth hearing. Some give words similar to Paul's that we can read today in the New Testament writings, such as, 'Absent from the body, present with the

Lord.' Another one says: 'To live for Christ – that is good; but to die, that's gain.' Another one says; 'To be with Christ is far better.'

All these are verses that are recorded in the New Testament as summarizing what Paul and other Christians were proclaiming throughout the Roman Empire and beyond. For everywhere they went, they did not proclaim some new ethic, some novel system of theology. The exhilaration, the exuberance of their proclamation was *'Jesus is alive'*, and soon many other men and women found themselves motivated by the same theme.

". . . buried with the hope that . . ."

Pumping hope in

Yes, *Jesus is alive*, and somehow or other, men and women who found that it was hard to face life, let alone death, discovered that they could face even death with this theme resounding in their hearts: *Jesus is alive*. Within twenty years of the execution of Jesus Christ (and probably even earlier) people were being buried with this affirmation written on their tombs. Certainly within thirty years of the crucifixion of that peasant leader from Galilee, Jesus of Nazareth – an artisan, a carpenter – men and women were being buried with the hope that somehow or other their death was not a dead end. They were buried believing that their death was not the culmination of a meaningless existence of loving, laughing, crying and denying, that they had experienced during their seventy years or even less.

". . . death was not a dead end."

Jesus' resurrection had pumped hope into the dead end of humanity, had pulsated meaning into the emptiness of our human existence. Taking the very dust of the grave he ordered it into a meaningful life saying: Death has been conquered; the victory has come; God has spoken to the world's greatest need; the last enemy has been defeated.

These first Christians said that Jesus had not just risen from death in some spiritual way, but had actually risen bodily from the grave; walked through a wall, true, but still appeared bodily to his disciples, convincing them he was there. He ate fish off a plate, presumably left the bones on the side, and walked out again. 'What was that?' they might ask. 'Was it a spirit or an apparition?' But when they picked up the bones from the side of the plate, they would say, 'That was for real!' These were the sorts of things that happened.

It was not a mystical kind of recycle like the crops that come year by year as the grain dies and comes in a new harvest. It was a resurrection showing that death had been beaten, and it put into the hearts and lives of men and women a concrete reason for their love, for their joy, for their self-denial, humility, peace, self-control: these were seen to be values which belong to a world which cannot be defeated, for it rose again in the person of Jesus Christ and continues for ever.

Believe it or not. Now we might conclude that these first-century people were less sophisticated, more gullible than we are today. But frankly I think they would have found it harder to believe in a resurrection than we do. Science has accustomed us to the amazing. You imagine saying to a first-century character, for instance, that if you watch a little box in somebody's front room you can see someone building a satellite station in space. He would have said, 'You are a lunatic; we don't believe that sort of stuff; you are not going to con us; we are good down-to-earth peasants; we know what life is all about.' If you had told them that somebody had risen from the grave, they would find it hard to believe. Don't forget that they would have seen lots of people die, would probably have a more first-hand experience of dead bodies than most of us, who veil its reality from ourselves by sophisticated civilized practices. They knew quite as well as we do, if not better, that people just don't rise again from death.

And yet, somehow or other they were convinced. Something that they claimed really had happened as an event in history, right down in the midst of our human scene; something which could eat fish and leave the bones on the side of the plate, had changed their whole attitude to life and to death.

dead or alive?

". . . you are not going to con us . . ."

The whole Christian message stands or falls upon this event in history. If Christ did not leave the grave, if Jesus never rose again, then our idealistic Christian hopes, our attempts at love and selflessness, are really empty and useless.

But if Christ did rise from the grave, says the apostle Paul, then our faith is not in vain. Our faith is empty unless Christ rose from the grave, but if Christ is risen then our faith has content. It is not a dream, a speculation, a wish, even a vision: it is *reality* based in time and space, written in the dust of the earth, spelt out in the blood of the cross and an empty grave, and then, and only then, driven experientially and subjectively into people's hearts. There is something real in history authenticating our experience. And so it is inevitable that from the first century to our present day, men and women have sought to destroy the Christian faith by attacking the resurrection of Jesus Christ, realizing that this is a fundamental plank upon which everything else stands or falls.

". . . somehow they were convinced."

Gilbert West. In the eighteenth century a couple of men decided, when they went up to Oxford, that they would share the attack between them. Lord Lyttleton would write a book to prove that the apostle Paul was never actually converted to Jesus Christ (a bold attempt, if nothing else!); the other man, Gilbert West, decided that he would attack the resurrection. So each set about his task, not meeting for some years.

When at last they met, and asked how each was getting on with his respective work, Lyttleton said, in effect, that he was sorry but he was just not going to get the book out. In fact, as he had studied the material to try and weigh up the case, he himself had been converted to Christ. He was sorry to disappoint his friend! Gilbert West replied that, as a matter of fact, he had written his book but it would be coming out as a book in *defence of the resurrection of Jesus*.

". . . one night he had an encounter . . ."

You can find the book today in the British Museum, and on the fly-leaf there is a quotation from the Book of Ecclesiasticus (in the Apocrypha), and it says, 'Don't judge a matter until you have examined it' – which is fairly useful advice, I think, when we seek to dismiss certain claims without ever looking at them.

F. Morison, Who Moved the Stone? (Faber, 1944)

Frank Morison. More recently in the twentieth century a journalist and lawyer, Frank Morison, took it upon himself to try to hit Christianity in its solar plexus, in order to see the whole thing fall. He tells us in the preface of his book *Who Moved the Stone?* that he set out writing the book to attack Christianity and destroy it by disproving the resurrection of Jesus Christ.

"We are not likely to be taken in easily . . ."

In order to be fair to the facts he had to read the material that was available on the subject, in particular the four gospels. As he weighed up the evidence placed before him in those writings he came to the conclusion that the case was a *bona fide* one, and he wrote his book supporting the fact of Christ's resurrection.

Jesus Christ said he was going to conquer death. He convinced those who thought he could not do it that he had, and he has gone on convincing people for 2,000 years since, that he has done what most of us would say is really the impossible. We are not likely to be taken in easily with that sort of stuff – unless it is real.

death – the real thing

Before we spend a little time trying to assess the evidence for this great event in history, let us consider the implications of death, because death is a problem. Don't let us try and hide from it. You know how it used to be: the Victorians would not discuss sex, the beginnings of life, but they were quite happy to talk about death. We, today, are absolutely obsessed with talking about the beginnings of life, but we dare not look death in the face. If we do, we have to cover it up in the most unrealistic way possible, to try to pretend it is not there. We hide behind sophisticated rituals and the expertise of professionals, to remove the evidence from our view.

"Victorians would not discuss sex . . ."

Alternatively, we condition ourselves with such a surfeit of television simulations of death that the real thing, if it should come near us, seems equally unreal. However, if even for a moment we break through this defence and let death's reality touch our lives, we instinctively know that if God has got nothing to say about death, in Jesus Christ, then our faith in him is redundant.

Unless a world-view can not only speak about death but also do something about it, it is futile from the outset. Only a faith built on such an answer is going to be adequately satisfying for this great problem. For death is a huge problem.

The moral problem

First, there is a *moral problem* with death. If life can come to such an abrupt and (some would claim) total end, then it throws into question the moral values everyone assumes. Is there any value in love, in self-denial, in sacrifice, if all that remains of these things, of

". . . we dare not look death in the face."

". . . a foetus that never comes to birth . . ."

our human choices, is a handful of dust in the end? The writer Camus tells us, 'That which exalts life to its highest is also that which degrades it to absurdity for it is all meaningless.' If death is the end, then our moral values are worth virtually nothing. Some have faced that presupposition and lived accordingly. But remember that the Christian God claims to meet this dilemma.

Imagine you could talk to a foetus in the womb of its mother, as it is developing little hands, eyes and feet. You might ask, 'Aren't you looking forward to the day when you come forth?'

'Oh no,' she could reply, 'it is much too nice in here.'

'But what about those little eyes that are developing in you?'

'Eyes? I can't see any eyes, in fact I can't see anything. Besides, it's dark; I don't need them.'

'What about those little hands?'

'I don't have to hold anything here.'

'What about those little feet?'

'I don't want to run around, thanks very much!'

'But there is a larger life coming,' you protest. 'There is something bigger and more meaningful for you.'

Similarly, there is a realm where values have meaning and existence, and it is virtually embryonic suicide, it is spiritual abortion, to ignore the reality that God has something larger after this scene for those moral values which we develop in life, growing moral hands, feet and eyes. We are like a foetus that never comes to birth, unless we discover that there is an answer to death, and there is a larger life. Christians claim that there is something which God has planned and prepared for those who, in Christ, go through from this scene into something bigger.

the philosophical problem

Then there is a philosophical problem. Since death is the one certain feature of life, we have to accommodate it in our world-view and it is a problem. In his book, *Dr Zhivago*, Pasternak grapples with the ugliness and problem of death. Zhivago as a little boy looks out of the window and remembers his mother. He sees her grave, tries to imagine her alive, and thinks, 'What does it all mean?' Pasternak says that centuries upon centuries of the best of human thought have grappled with the meaning of death, if perhaps we might come up ultimately with the solution, and be able to conquer it. Thus he puts it over in his novel. It is a philosophical problem.

Sartre tells us that all we can do about death is to face it fully in our experience, and come out the other side into a 'horrible calm', as though the very nemesis of it has overtaken our system and life is to be lived in the horrible calm of its ultimate doom. H. G. Wells says, 'If there is no larger life after death, then this life is a huge ugly joke. Man is like an ass braying across the scenes of history.' Is there no answer philosophically?

". . . life is a huge ugly joke."

Discover more. Sartre and Wells certainly sound a different note from those who have gone to their deaths with a conviction, even an exhilaration, which somehow or other seems to suggest that they have discovered something more.

For instance, there was a man in the Reformation period who was sentenced to death by burning. As his sentence was read out in the courts, he broke forth singing one of the Old Testament songs, Psalm 122: 'I was glad when they said to me, "Let us go into the house of the Lord!" ' Well now, someone like that is quite beyond it; you can't do much with him; he starts to sing when you tell him that he is going to die! Either he is terribly deluded, mentally deranged, or he has got hold of something.

Osment tells us in her little book that, as a convinced Communist, she was quite happy with the system until she was confronted by death, her mother's death. Then she began to ask questions which her Communist world-view did not answer. It had nothing to say about this most certain of all life's experiences. She was encouraged therefore to seek further, and discovered Jesus Christ. Death is a philosophical problem, and we need a world-view that covers all experiences.

The psychological problem

Death is a psychological problem, for everybody fears death. I have met and counselled many people who have suffered from depression and fear following the death of someone close to them. I remember one such young woman whom I met while doing some pastoral visiting in a village. She had not slept well nor been able to go out or care for her child properly for months following the death of her mother. She simply could not shake off the fearful depression that hung over her.

I talked with her and read to her the story of Jesus Christ walking on the Sea of Galilee and coming to his disciples in their fear, saying 'It is I. Do not be afraid.' (They had thought he was a ghost or something supernatural from beyond the grave.) When they received him into their boat, they came immediately to the place they had been trying to reach. Then I told this young woman, 'The Lord Jesus does not want you to fear. In fact, the most commanded thing in the Bible is "Fear not". Let's ask God to meet you in this problem.' So we prayed.

When I saw this young woman the next day, she was completely transformed. Her eyes were peaceful and bright. She had found that the living Lord Jesus is able to deal with the psychological problem of death. Now she wanted to know how she could find a lasting, eternal relationship with God.

Facing death. Professor Jung, one of the fathers of modern psychology, said there was no-one over the age of thirty-five who was not living with either a conscious or unconscious fear of death. Of course, like much psychological theory, you can't really test it. For if you said to Jung, 'I don't have a fear of death', he could say, 'But you have – it is suppressed, that's why you don't notice it.' Yet his years of seeking to help people in their deepest psychological problems suggest that this great man in psychiatry should be listened to. We all live with a fear of death,

"We live with a fear of death."

particularly if we have passed the mid-point of our seventy years!

the religious problem

"Buddha, Mohammed, Confucius . . . all have their tombs . . ."

There is what we might call a *religious problem* in death. For the great world leaders of religion, in all their sincerity and for all the truths that they may have lighted on, still had nothing to say to us about death, in any demonstrable form. Buddha, Mohammed, Confucius, Karl Marx . . . all have their tombs at which you can go and pay your respects.

Jesus Christ hasn't! There is no shrine for him. He has no tomb. In fact, we are not even quite sure where it was they put him when they crucified him, for nobody cared too much afterwards. Why go to find a tomb when you can find him alive? You don't go to look amongst the dead for the living.

There is a religious problem, a religious problem that exists and is not answered, either, by some eerie voice from a mediumistic trance. Will any vague voice from some distant shadow-realm convince us that there is a life after the grave? We want something solid, in flesh, with the smell of the early morning on it, the dew and the dust of the earth; and that is how the body of Jesus was when he broke out of the grave on that morning. He came and ate with his disciples. There was earthly reality about it.

Now these are various areas of the problem. If God has nothing to say through the Christian message about the universal experience of death, nothing, I mean, which has a real integral base to it, then really we have no message for a dying world.

Death may have its value in reminding us that we are not independent creatures. Drinking a drop of cyanide, or holding on to the end of a high-voltage cable, will soon convince us of that truth! We are not creatures independent of our Creator and death will remind us that there is this problem in our life which needs to be dealt with, to which death is but the final conclusion. For if I deny my dependent humanity, I write my own suicide certificate. Death may even be a mercy, for there must be many people who, when confronted with it, think again.

The answer to the problem of death lies in the physical resurrection of Jesus Christ, giving hope that as Jesus was raised from the dead so also God will raise those who trust in him. The resurrection of Jesus is central to the Christian faith and to the path to God. So what evidence do we have of its authenticity?

THE CORPSE IS MISSING

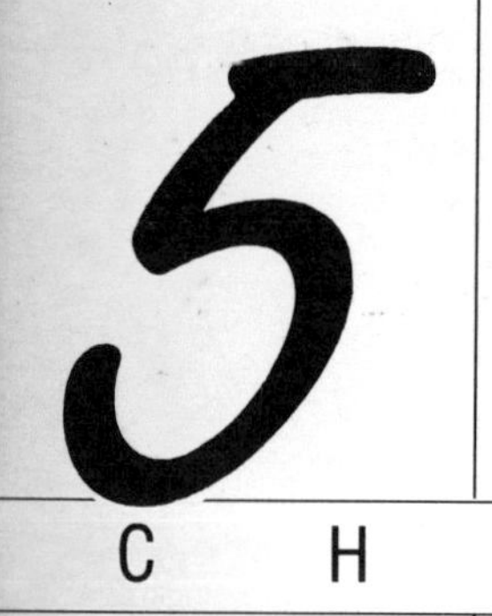

CHAPTER

The first question that must be answered is: If Jesus did not rise from death, then what happened to his corpse? There seems no doubt that the body of Jesus was missing from his tomb three days after his death. This was an accepted fact at the time as evidenced by two things:

No 'empty tomb' was preached

"There seems no doubt . . ."

When the first disciples began to preach the message of Jesus after his ascension, they did not once refer to his empty tomb. They said, 'Jesus is alive!' 'Jesus is at the centre of the universe', 'he is taking over all things', but they did not try to argue that his tomb was empty, because it was already a widely known fact. All their hearers *knew* that something had happened to the body of Jesus; the apostles needed only to proclaim, 'God has raised him from the dead!'

". . . what happened to it?"

No shrine

If it were *not* for the resurrection message it might surprise us that there is no shrine for Christianity, made from the tomb of Jesus, at which his followers could express their devotion and respect. Despite the fact that thousands were healed or helped by him, or heard his teaching and acclaimed him, yet none seemed to desire a memorial by which to honour him. 'Why seek for the living among the dead?' His followers didn't.

If we accept the fact that Jesus' body was missing from his tomb, we have to ask what happened to it? Perhaps the most popular theory is that the body was stolen. There were several groups who might have had a motive for stealing the body, so we will examine them one by one.

Stolen body theory

The first objection that was made to the claims of the Christians in the first century was that his *disciples* had stolen Jesus' body from the tomb. You can find this in Matthew's Gospel: the guards were paid off to report this story. It is recorded again in

(Matthew 28:11–15)

the Jewish Talmud: Jesus Christ's body was removed from the tomb by the disciples. Is this a reasonable explanation?

"Is this a reasonable explanation?"

Was it the disciples? Is it reasonable, first, that a bunch of men who fled when Christ was apprehended and who didn't even stay for his trial were going to go to the only tomb in the whole of Jerusalem that was guarded by soldiers trained in war? Is it reasonable that they were going to try to overwhelm the guards and take the body of Jesus for some unknown reason? And what would they do with it? How were they to get rid of that body of Jesus? (If you have ever tried to get rid of a body you will know it is extremely difficult!) They would have had to get rid of the body and then go around the place saying 'Jesus is alive'.

Is it psychologically possible that those shattered men could find it in themselves at last to stand up before a vast crowd and begin to proclaim that Christ was really alive? Ethically speaking, is it possible, without having a psychological breakdown to stand up and proclaim to men and women throughout the world, 'This is the message we have: love your neighbour, turn the other cheek, don't tell lies', all on the basis that the story of Christ rising from the grave is the biggest lie yet? And then to die for it!

Is it feasible that the Christian message could have spread so rapidly with these disadvantages? Moreover, not one of those men squealed that they knew of any other story!

". . . is it possible . . ."

Yet the authorities would have paid them off well (and every man has his price). They would have loved to have got evidence that the body really had been stolen; and yet not one of those disciples (and it ran into hundreds who saw Jesus alive, maybe thousands) ever split on the event, *because they were convinced they had seen the Lord alive*. The tomb really was empty, but not because the disciples had stolen the body.

Was it thieves? If it were not the disciples who robbed the tomb, could it not have been *thieves*? Thieves? Going to the only guarded tomb in Jerusalem, when there were plenty of others they could have rifled, to rifle the tomb of the poorest man that had walked through those streets?

When Jesus wanted to talk about a coin he had to say, 'Has anybody got a penny?' and they gave it to him from the crowd, and he held it up, had something to say, and then, presumably gave it back. And he had the most interesting way of paying his taxes – but I will leave those of you with the same problem to find that one out!

"... evidence that the body ... had been stolen ..."

(See Matthew 17:27)

'The poorest man in Jersualem has just been buried, let us go and break the official seal and get to his tomb!' So the thieves risked their lives, and then left all the valuables behind. The graveclothes were neatly wrapped up together and left, and so were the costly spices. Nothing was taken except the body, and what can you do with that?

Was it the authorities? Could it then have been the *authorities* who removed the corpse, anticipating perhaps a bit of an uprising? 'Those Galileans are hot-headed, after too much drink on a festival occasion, they might, now that their leader has gone, start causing some trouble. Well, the best thing to do is to shift the body away from the shrine that they are bound to make out of the tomb; and then we will have the whole thing under control!'

Frankly, I think that would be the best way to start a riot, not to quell one. If they were hot-headed Galileans, to shift the body would be to them the last indignity to be given to their great leader. No, that was the very thing likely to cause a riot.

Anyway, if for some other reason they removed the body from the tomb, surely it would have been the simplest thing in the world to have exposed the body when these men began to proclaim that Jesus was alive.

They would have loved to have had the body somewhere, so that they could have produced it. For *they* were the ones accused; they had taken the Jewish Christ and executed him, as the apostles were proclaiming. If the authorities had stolen the body, why didn't they say so and produce it when the Christians were claiming Jesus had risen?

Was it someone else? Even less probable is the suggestion that some lesser, *nondescript disciples* stole the body and deceived the leaders. But again, not a breath of such a suspicion ever existed in the early Christian community. Neither would the scepticism of a Thomas have been overcome by mere hearsay of lesser people. The same could also be said of the rest of the leadership. The leading apostles not only saw an empty tomb, but they also saw Jesus after the resurrection.

". . . likely to cause a riot."

Mistaken tomb theory

Perhaps the tomb was a *mistaken* one – you know, early in the morning, Mary Magdalene, rather emotional, with lots of tears in her eyes. It's rather misty and she doesn't know Jerusalem; she goes to the wrong tomb, and there she meets a gardener. The gardener says, 'He is not here.' She thinks he said, 'He is risen.' She rushes back and tells Peter. Peter goes running out, and he finds the wrong tomb too, and so does John. Joseph of Arimathea then hears, and the tomb is in his own garden, but he also goes to the wrong one!

"Nobody was going to believe that sort of story . . ."

And don't forget that the garden in which Jesus was buried would have been something like Hampstead Heath or Central Park on a Bank Holiday as soon as it started to get around that Jesus was risen! Nobody was going to believe that sort of story without putting their heads inside the sepulchre themselves, for everybody in Jerusalem knew it was being claimed that Jesus was alive. Surely not everybody in Jerusalem would find the wrong tomb and leave the right one, guarded, totally uninvestigated?

Fainting theory

Perhaps Christ only *fainted* on the cross and came round in the tomb when the cool air swept through. Being revived, he pushed the stone away in his physically wrecked conditon – a stone which a group of women couldn't move – and appeared to his disciples, absolutely clapped out, with hands and feet bleeding, and his side marked from the spear thrust, and convinced them that he was the Prince of Life who had conquered death. He then staggered out to let the whole hoax go on, and presumably to meet Paul on the Damascus Road, before disappearing into India or somewhere and from history.

This theory appears in a more sophisticated form in Dr Schonfield's book, *The Passover Plot*, where Jesus is depicted on the cover as a puppet with strings. In actual fact, says Schonfield, Jesus believed in the power of God, nevertheless he staged the whole crucifixion, because he believed sincerely that the Leader of Israel, the Messiah, must suffer according to the Scripture, but also return to reign.

". . . why did he have to play-act the crucifixion?"

Well, we might ask, if he believed sincerely in the power of God, why did he have to play-act the crucifixion? God's power surely could be believed to cope with a resurrection as much as with anything else, especially if it were so certain that it was prophesied in the Scriptures.

Also, it might be asked why it was that only two minor disciples were in on this secret plan, *i.e.* to pretend he was dead and then to revive him so that he could reign, namely, Joseph of Arimathea and Nicodemus. Christ was supposed to have been drugged only, by the anodyne offered at the crucifixion, which the gospel writers say he refused.

The fact was, says Schonfield, the plot failed because the soldier thrust his spear into Christ's side and really dealt a death blow. Schonfield, twenty centuries later, says that despite the spear wound, Jesus did come round in the tomb before he expired and sent messages to Peter, James and John via Joseph and Nicodemus, that they were to preach the good news in all the world. And that was sufficient to convince the apostles that he was alive!

Such a glaring contradiction in the whole reconstruction of the story, that is, to say Jesus believed in God's power yet still felt he had to play-act at death, should surely have been avoided by such a close thinker as Dr Schonfield.

Besides the fact of the empty tomb, we have the claims of the first disciples that they *saw Jesus risen*. Some have ascribed this to hallucinations.

Hallucination theory

If the Lord Jesus did not faint, then was it perhaps possible that people had *hallucinations*, thinking that they saw him? 'You know women, they are a bit prone to these things; Mary of Magdalene, for instance, she was that type! They are very emotional.'

But it wasn't only women, it was hard-headed fishermen, tax-collectors (I wish my tax-collector would have a few hallucinations!) It was not just women by themselves, or men by themselves; it was whole groups of people. It was not just in the morning, or in the afternoon, or in the evening; it was all times of the day.

Most people suffering from hallucinations find that if the visions die away, they do so gradually as time goes on, becoming less and less frequent. But these appearances of Jesus happened for forty days only and then they stopped suddenly for everybody. It was not likely to be hallucinations that gave rise to the resurrection story, and anyway they could not account for the empty tomb.

Legends

Of course the stories could be just *legends*, surely, one must allow that! There are legends that have grown up around all great people. Jesus was a great healer; he had done many miracles; surely legendary figures like this are bound to get stories attached to them.

But the material we have hardly appears legendary. The apostle Paul tells us, having been converted within three to five years of the crucifixion, that he received this message, 'that Christ had died according to the Scriptures, and rose again'. Three or even five years is not very long for some fanciful story to attach itself around a popular leader.

(1 Corinthians 15:1–8)

Moreover, if you read the New Testament, you don't find the atmosphere of legends: most of the writings are given in a factual way, within some thirty or forty years of the events. They are written as from eye-witnesses, and these eye-witnesses report, and their reports integrate, as people who have been in the event and seen these things.

". . . legends, surely, one must allow that!"

If you were writing a legend, you could not have resisted more detail about the actual resurrection itself, could you? The shaking and the quivering of the body, that is bound to turn your readers on! The movement of the clothes, the upheaval in the tomb – you could not have left out all that!

Yet not a word is said. Why? because nobody saw it. They wrote only what they saw. Peter and James had private interviews with Jesus after the resurrection. Would you not have liked to have heard what happened when Peter saw Jesus? 'Well, Peter, so you denied me, did you? I suppose you will need forgiveness . . . *etc.*' – you would love to have heard it all, and seen Peter really put in his place!

". . . that is bound to turn your readers on!"

Even more interesting would be a scene when Jesus confronted his unbelieving half-brother James. Not a word said about it, just that these interviews happened; we don't know, fortunately, the personal context. The bits that we would have loved if we were writing legends are just not there.

Added to this, what legend from the first century would say that the first apostle (meaning 'one who is sent') to the apostles was a woman? Mary Magdalene was sent, 'Go and tell my brothers.' First-century legends of that calibre would never have got off the ground when there were no Women's movements around.

There are the accounts. Nondescript disciples like Cleopas, on the road back from Emmaus, come back to Jerusalem and tell how they have met the Lord. Would legend record the unbelief of the big-time apostles, and Thomas in particular?

I remember once in a university someone coming up to talk to me after a meeting, looking over my shoulder as I was reading a passage of the Bible. He said, 'Hey, this fellow Matthew is *not* trying to con us, is he? Look, he puts down here that when Jesus

(*Matthew 28:17*)

appeared, some of his disciples didn't believe in him. If Matthew had been trying to con us he would not have put that in, would he?' We have got the factual accounts. They don't read like fairy stories, written up later as legends, but historical eye-witness documents.

the fact of the matter

Apart from the seven objections to the resurrection which we have dealt with above, there are seven positive points which add their reasonableness to the case for the resurrection.

". . . the case for the resurrection."

1. *The Old Testament* said it would happen, foreshadowing it by men such as Isaac and Jonah received back from the dead, by its inference that the 'suffering servant' would reign as King for ever and ever, and by explicit prophecies concerning the resurrection of Christ in Psalms, Isaiah and Hosea.

2. *Christ* taught that it would happen, although his disciples record that they did not believe him. He said he must suffer many things at the hands of the leaders, and on the third day rise again.

3. *The disciples,* after the resurrection, believed, and said he did do it, and they would have taken more convincing than any.

4. *Sunday* became the day on which the Christians met to worship, whereas the sabbath as God's day had been written into the Jew for over 1,200 years. It needed such a trauma as a rising from the dead to give the first day of the week a greater significance than the sabbath.

5. *The message* was 'Jesus is alive', not an

abstract philosophical or theological concept. The disciples didn't preach 'God is love' and 'Love your neighbour' – at least, not at first—but that God had done something powerful in history. Yes, 'Jesus is alive.'

6, *Today* all over the world there are men and women who say: We have found that our experience that Christ is alive can be interpreted and attested only by this event in history. The two accord – the living Christ today in our lives and what happened in world history 2,000 years ago. The existence of the church is substantial evidence, for it is not a philosophical society of learning, or a religious club, but a community based on the assertion that Christ is risen.

7. *Eternal life*. Above all those things, if Jesus really were who he claimed to be, God speaking to us in our sufferings, and in our death, if Jesus really were God, should we be surprised that this irresistible resurrecting God breaks out of the tomb we gave him and starts to show us he is alive? Eternal life has this kind of permanence. He does it when we try to bury him in our subconscious too.

I remember one atheist looking almost neurotic and saying to me when I asked if he ever thought of God, 'I never *stop* thinking about God!' Of course, because God is alive in Christ seeking to make himself known.

In the resurrection God really did beat the grave. The apostle Paul sums it up like this: ' "Death is swallowed up in victory." "O death, where is thy victory? O death, where is thy sting?" The sting of death is sin, and the power of sin is the law. But thanks be to God, who gives us the victory through our Lord Jesus Christ.'

(1 Corinthians 15:54–57)

". . . substantial evidence . . ."

removing the sting

". . . a child is bitten by a snake."

An Indian friend of mine tells how he saw a woman, devoted to her child, snatch it up when it had been bitten by a snake. She proceeded to bite, then suck the wound drawing the poison out and into herself. She died, but the child lived.

Now the 'sting of death', that is its fear and pain, is sin. The strength of that sin is the law, that God condemns sin. We know we're sinners, and sin stings and bites into our beings. But Christ has sucked the sting, swallowed death, tasted death for every woman and man. He borrowed our death because he had no death on his own account; he borrowed our death in order to finish with it so that we might live. He died that we might live.

(See Hebrews 2:9)

A Christian in a Nazi concentration camp spoke to a Jewess about Jesus. She reacted, 'Jesus died for me but I don't understand it, I don't get it. How do you mean, Jesus died for me? It doesn't make sense.' One day she was in a queue of people with her towel over her arm, her number on it. She thought she was going to the washrooms. Unknown to her, it was the gas chamber!

"A Christian in a Nazi concentration camp . . ."

The Christian saw her standing there. She sensed that the whole crowd of Jews was being deceived into death. She said, 'Excuse me, would you mind running back to the billet, I have left my soap there? I will hold your towel and your place.' When the Jewess came back the queue had moved in. The Christian woman had died in her place. That Jewess actually came out of the camp under the other woman's name and number. She had begun to understand how Christ had died for her.

The unlikely convert. I know a man who was, for a large part of his life, an atheist. He was a member of the Communist party, until Hungary was suppressed. He left the Communist party like many at that time on conscience grounds, saying, 'Whatever life is about it certainly cannot help mankind to act in these ways. I must look further.' He was a first-class scientist, a doctor of chemistry. Finding that most of his work was going into atomic war-heads, he left the research industry and became a school-teacher (his pay dropped, of course!).

One day he was asked by his headmaster to speak at school assembly. He answered to this effect: 'I'm sorry, Sir, but I haven't an ounce of religion in me.' 'Don't let that worry you,' the headmaster said, 'just tell them that science has made the universe so big that we, therefore, are so small we ought to be humble.' He agreed to have a go at it because, after all, he didn't want to lose another job! He tried to tell the school in that particular morning assembly that science had made the world and universe so big and humanity was so small, therefore we ought to be humble. He didn't think he had done too well (neither did anyone else!).

". . . it was very cool, straightforward and plain."

The following week a local minister came to the school; he himself had only recently made the astounding discovery that Jesus really is alive. He gave a good talk about being humble because Christ has beaten our biggest problem, death, and if we call him Lord, then we can begin to find the answer to other problems. But, of course, you have to be humble to call him Lord.

The science teacher was very impressed

J. N. D. Anderson, The Evidence for the Resurrection *(IVP, 1950)*

with what he heard. Approaching the minister afterward, he said, 'Can you tell me any more about this? Have you anything more I can read about it?' The minister took from his pocket a little booklet called *The Evidence for the Resurrection*.

That evening the teacher went through the pamphlet and decided that it was very cool, straightforward and plain, and as a scientist, since the facts seemed pretty strong, he ought to do something about it for it seemed to present a good case.

That night he got his wife's Bible and began to read. He read on right through till the morning, then went to school and announced himself in the staff room as a Christian. The only evidence he could show them were the bags under his eyes – he had been up all night!

Two days later the school religious instruction master came to his home and said, 'We are very surprised that you have become a Christian after all these years; after all, we know your background and your atheism. I expect you don't really know much about Christianity?' He replied, 'No, I don't really, but do come in.' So the Scripture master explained all sorts of difficulties about being a Christian.

". . . difficulties about being a Christian."

After some of these difficulties, as he saw them, had been spelt out about the Bible and Christ, the science master replied: 'I'm very sorry, I haven't really followed much of what you have been saying, as I have only been a Christian two days, but one thing I do know is, *Jesus is alive, isn't he?'*

the living God

Jesus is alive, isn't he? Jesus' dying on the cross takes the sting out of death because it deals with the problem of sin itself, yours and mine, that we might begin to discover in our experience a *living God – a God who is alive*, as alive as a man who has burst forth out of the grave. It is that Christ who is the Christ of Christianity.

In the last book of the Bible, Jesus is depicted as standing at the door of our lives, knocking. We feel this knocking when we sense that we should respond to God. When we know that God is saying something to us, then he knocks. 'Behold, I stand at the door and knock; if any one hears my voice and opens the door, I will come in to him and eat with him': I will live with that person. This is the offer and the promise of the living Lord Jesus to any who begin to sense that there is a knocking at their lives.

"It is the hand of God . . ."

Perhaps God has been knocking for some while. We have ignored it; we have not faced up to whose hand is knocking. It is the hand of God revealed in Christ, asking us to respond by the exposure of our lives to him, saying, 'Please come in; take over; begin to deal with me in a living way, not only to meet the problem of death, but the problem of life itself, the problem of my need and my sin. Please come in.'

'Behold, I stand at the door and knock; if any one hears my voice and opens the door, I will come in' – It is a promise, *I will*, full of power, for he is *alive*!

(Revelation 3:20)

THE BEAUTIFUL PEOPLE

C H A P T E R

We take a very significant step forward in getting involved with God when we come to realize that God is not very interested in nice people – well, no more interested in them than in anyone else. It is emancipating to discover that God's interest is in men and women just as they are and wherever they are.

"If you happen to be a 'nice' type . . ."

God is not particularly partial to those who might have been fortunate enough to have had a nice background, balanced upbringing, plenty of good inheritance genes so that they can swing into life on all cylinders and be psychologically very well forward in the *avant garde* of human advance.

Thank God he is not interested only in them, for the majority of the human race is not like that. Most people have been somewhat battered in their psychology, have had shattering traumas when children, have had to hassle with all sorts of quirks in their sex life. They have been brought up with views of life which nurtured strange ideas and cramped their minds – that is, if they have ever had the energy to think at all, having had less than enough to eat.

"What must I do . . ."

If you happen to be a 'nice' type, then you are fortunate – that is what it amounts to really – because the majority of people just haven't got that head start in life.

Rich people

One day a man came to Jesus Christ who really was very 'nice' indeed. He was a rich man, and that usually helps you to be nice. He was in government too, and of course having influence over others is always handy to keep you on a well-balanced keel. He had been well brought up, so much so that Jesus virtually commended him that he had not lied, and he didn't oppress others, he was not a murderer, he didn't steal, he wasn't the sort of man who would break the basic laws of morality. Nonetheless, the man knew that there was something missing and asked: 'What must I do to inherit eternal life?'

(Luke 18:18–25)

Now, of course, eternal life is that life that belongs to God, so to possess it means getting involved with God. But how do I get involved with God? Jesus' reply was: 'Sell what you have and come, follow me.' 'Get involved with me,' says Jesus, for Christ is eternal life, and Christ is what God is doing in this world.

Christ is God's own eternal life pumped into humanity to get them moving in his stream of things. So, the reply of Jesus was: 'Get rid of what you have inherited; get rid of your past back-log; get rid of your advantages and privileges; forget your hereditary genes which have served you so well, and pitch everything into a total, new abandonment to the life of God. Come, follow me.' The young man was a 'nice' person, but Jesus was not too interested in that. His call to and for all people is 'Ditch the riches of your psychology, your mentality, your past, and come. Come just as you are, poor, in need, spiritually bankrupt, and get involved with what Jesus Christ is offering you – eternal life.'

"I have never murdered. I have never stolen."

religious people

(Luke 18:9–14)

Jesus told a story about two people, one of whom was very religious. They went up to the temple to pray, and the religious one said: 'Thank you, God, that I give you a tenth of everything that I have and that I even fast, denying myself for others. I thank you that I am not an extortioner – I'm a very good employer; you go and ask my friends! I don't cheat people. I have never murdered. I have never stolen, and I have kept the commandments quite well really!'

Then he looked sideways, and to his disgust found that somebody else had crept in to the religious meeting in the temple. It was one of those nasty, corrupt types who was a quisling, sold out to the foreign government that was in power, and making quite a good racket out of it too – a tax-collector! And this man in the corner was beating his chest and crying: 'O God, be merciful to me; I am bankrupt as far as you are concerned!'

So, looking across at him, and then quickly away again of course, the first man, the Pharisee, continued to pray: 'I thank you, God, that I am not like that tax-collector!' 'After all,' he implied, 'you must be very pleased to have a friend as good as me when characters like that are around!'

Such a nich person!

The Pharisee was a nice sort. He himself was certain of it and others doubtless thought so too. He was the kind of person you like to work for. I like to work for somebody who does not use extortion and oppress me, don't you? I like someone who is not an adulterer, especially if my daughter is around, don't you? And I certainly like somebody who is going to pay 100 pence to the pound and fork out a bit for charity occasionally. The Pharisee was all this and told God so in his prayer, in case the Almighty had forgotten.

But you see, Jesus was not too interested in the nice person as such; he seemed more interested in the wretch who was beating his chest and saying: 'There are all sorts of ugly, filthy, twisted things inside me, and I need help.' That is the man who got involved with God. For Jesus said: '[He] was in the right with God when he went home', which means not only *right* with him, but right *with* him, and involved with him. He can do something with a woman or man like that in this world.

> ". . . the soul stands naked before God."

Stripped bare. In the final analysis, when someone is stripped of all his or her psychological advantages and stands as a naked soul before God, then we see the real person. When the soul stands naked before God, the final, fundamental decisions of the spirit will be revealed – the things that we really chose; the things that we really ached for and wanted to be; the decisions we made about life but did not find the power to effect.

This is the real final person that lies inside and which will stand before God. It is in this that God is interested. At that final time we will have sloughed off all that we, happily perhaps, or maybe unhappily, happened to inherit as our psychological backlog.

That is why you can point at so many Christians and say, 'They are not particularly "nice" people.' No, not yet. They have a long way to go; they started with a lot of disadvantages and lack of privileges. And that is why you can look at some non-Christians and think, 'They are very, very nice folk.' Yes, they are swinging into life quite well. But they would be a lot different again if they came to the point of acknowledging that they need something else, something which God calls eternal life – his life, which means getting involved with him.

He showed us how it could be because he put that life in Christ, when Christ came to this world. He revealed eternal life as a person, so that we, mere people, could get involved with God. His life then becomes the very power and the pulse of our being and moves us out into the world in God's way and in God's movement.

"... so many Christians ... are not particularly 'nice' people."

Simply perfect

All this is not to say, of course, that a Christian is not to become – well, something better than 'nice'. Ultimately God is concerned to make us perfect. 'Be perfect, as your heavenly Father is perfect.' 'He sends rain on the just and on the unjust' – perfect towards everybody. Christ has set himself that task. When the rich young ruler came to him, Jesus said: 'If you want to be perfect, you lack one thing. Get rid of your inheritance and come, follow me – we will do things together.' It is perfection that God is after, not nice people. We may take a long while getting there, but that is what he wants.

(Matthew 5:48 and 45)

(See Luke 18:22)

But perhaps we are not prepared to let God so deal with us that we become perfect men and women, because we don't really like the idea of becoming perfect. We don't mind the idea of being nice; everyone will say: 'They are beautiful people; they are lovely people!' But to become perfect, that is a different matter altogether. That means putting your hands into the trouble. It means getting a bit stained with suffering. It means getting involved with sacrifice and self-denial. I'm not quite sure that I'm willing for that sort of call. 'Come, be perfect – as your heavenly Father is perfect.'

C. S. Lewis likens it to when you have

toothache as a child: you go to bed and bite the tooth and hope that the pain will go. You know that if you went to Mum she would give you an aspirin and it would be all right, but then, next morning, there would be more treatment to follow – you would be packed off to the dentist, and he would start tinkering around with all the other teeth, and they would all start to ache, even those that hadn't ached before! Then there is the drill! Consequently, you don't tell Mum. You try to put up with the little inconvenience and make it slightly less painful, because you know you would get the whole works if you got involved with Mother, and the dentist too.

The problem with Jesus. There is the same problem with Jesus Christ. When we get involved with him, it is the whole works that he is committed to – this perfection which he is working towards. Not just tinkering around with the odd tooth, but a thorough examination; then the removal of the corruption, and the packing back in of something else which is going to make us able to bite hard into life. He is going to make us perfect, because there really is a perfect world that is going to come. Jesus promised it and even said that it was 'at hand' – just around the corner.

(Matthew 4:17)

It is God's kingdom, the kingdom of righteousness, justice, peace, love. It is for this kingdom men and women are being prepared and trained. That is the kingdom to which we are moving if we are involved with the life of God. And that is the kingdom for which we have to be prepared, by becoming perfect ourselves, by getting hold of this perfect life that Christ is offering.

This is what a Christian is: Someone who is in the movement of what God is doing through this world, moving towards his perfection; someone who has received God's own life into himself and is in tune with the sphere of existence which God is going to bring on earth. The Christian lays hold of the values that belong to that kingdom even now, and starts to express them even before the final revolution comes.

Although there may not be very many nice Christians around yet, when the life of Christ which has got inside them has done its full work, when they have been stripped of all their inherent selfishness which they will be only too pleased to shed, just to look at them will make you want to fall down and worship. Just to look at them will make you want to say: 'What a magnificent thing!' Yes, that is what God is doing. A new kingdom will be born and there will be men and women who have been born for it because they have God's own life.

". . . a perfect world . . . just around the corner."

Getting started

Now as we have been thinking of the implications of the Christian faith, no doubt some of you have been beginning to say: 'Well, how can this particular encounter that you talk about, this getting involved with God, this being wrapped up with his life and with his person, how can this actually happen to me? How can I be involved with this movement of God, this "perfection trip" if you like? How can a person begin to know God?'

"I have reasoned it out."

There are three ways (which can sometimes be three difficulties) that I want to highlight, for there are many who want to know how such an encounter with Jesus Christ really can take place in their experience.

Knowing

If I meet somebody I might say: 'I know that woman', because I have met her. But how can I say I know God, or for that matter, how can I say I know anything? There are three factors involved:

- We can know something because *an authority* has told us. He has given us his testimony, and we believe his authority.
- Another way is to use *our reason*. We think as hard as we can until we say: 'Now I know – it is reasonable; I have reasoned it out.'
- We can know by *experience*; *e.g.* I know that there are animals that carry babies around in their pockets because I have been to Australia and I've seen such creatures!

These three factors usually interplay upon each other in order to help us to *know* something; for example, when you were a child your mother told you not to put your fingers in the fire or they would get burned. Furthermore she put a guard round the fire to make quite sure you couldn't experiment. You had to accept Mother's *authority* on the matter; after all, mothers are right about most things.

Besides, as you grew older and more observant, you noticed that things that were put on the fire usually went up in smoke! *Reason* told you it was probable that fire could burn fingers also.

The day came however when you stumbled near an unguarded fire, put your hand out to save yourself and . . . *experience* confirmed your mother's authority and your own reasoning in an unforgettable way. You really know now about fire burning fingers.

Christian knowledge. Similarly, when you find the path and become a Christian, you have usually considered the *authority* of God's Word and the testimony of other Christians; you may be convinced by your *reason* that God exists and is worth knowing, that you are a rebel cut off from God's life, needing forgiveness; that Jesus died to make possible your recovery and restoration and offers you his risen life.

Now comes the moment when you have to use *experience*. So you pray; you admit your need; you ask for forgiveness and a new relationship with God; you commit yourself.

You may not immediately experience anything much, but sense dictates that you persevere and see that the conditions are right; you approach God humbly and willing to do his will, prepared to forgive and love all men, ready to make changes and most of all to make God the most important thing in your life, to spend time *getting to know* him. The ensuing days begin to demonstrate to you that the authority you followed was right, and your reason was right: now your experience confirms it and you can say, 'I *know*.' His life has begun to work in you.

". . . fingers in the fire . . . get burned."

So if you are saying to yourself, 'How can I know that I am a Christian?', 'How can I really know that God has given me this eternal life?' then you have, perhaps, reached this step of knowing by experience. You have thought hard about the Christian faith; now comes the point where you must offer yourself personally to God.

Seeing

But there is another way we can talk about this encounter. Sometimes we say, 'Oh, I *see* now.' Maybe I have been looking at what it means to be a Christian; I have been examining the claims; I have been thinking hard: but somehow or other, it just does not seem to come alive to me.

"Now . . . you have to use experience."

Imagine yourself in a hut in a garden. You shut the door and it is pitch black except for one beam of light coming through a crack in the shed wall. You look at the beam of light – you can measure it, you can perhaps ascertain its intensity; you can see some other things by it, as you put them in its path. In that way you stand apart and examine the whole thing objectively.

But there comes a moment, as you move across the hut from one position to another, when you stand in that beam of light that is pouring in, and you look along it, upwards, out into the fuller light, and see the trees, the birds, the clouds, the sky, and then the sun, millions of miles away. A whole new world opens up and you now say, 'I know that light in another way from the way I knew it when I measured it and determined its intensity.' You have changed your position and it has become something experimental.

To know a person, too, one has to reach that particular stage. It means more than facts and figures – age, sex, height and colour of hair. It means spending time with that person and discovering what they think, how they react, what they value most highly. It also means seeing *ourselves* as the other person sees us – and that is sometimes an unpleasant surprise! It means, without in any sense changing who we are, at the same time being able to put ourselves in their shoes, think their thoughts, see things with their perspective, react as they would react. Any deep relationship involves becoming *like* the other person in this way, at least to some degree.

"A whole new world opens up . . ."

Standing in the light. And this is what it means to become a Christian. We get involved with God. We put ourselves in his searching light and admit our failures and need. We feel the warming light of his promised forgiveness and new life. We spend time listening to what he has to say in the words specially preserved for us in the Bible. Here we see more of God and more of ourselves. We speak to him (what we usually call praying) and are ready for what he may want to say to us, too. Standing in the light he has provided for us, we can look out on the world and really see it, for the first time, with his perspective. And we will see a whole new life coming into view.

This life is also seen in others. It was perfectly expressed in Jesus who was the 'living image' of God. But as Christ lives in other believers we see in them the fulfilment of God's design when he made man in his own image. And thus we see God in other people. Our Christian life becomes a further knowing of him in the fellowship of his people.

". . . a whole new life comes into view."

believing

"But I haven't got enough faith."

Thirdly, perhaps some of you say, 'But I haven't got enough faith. You have to have faith to become a Christian, and I haven't got it!' Well, it is true, if you are going to have a relationship with *anybody* you have to have a certain amount of faith: faith that the look on their face is to some degree a true reflection of what is going on inside; faith that the words they use are a genuine expression, to some extent, of what they want to say.

To meet God too you have to have a certain amount of faith. But with many of us our trouble is this, instead of majoring on the little bit of faith that is always necessary for a relationship, we focus on the doubts, and we build on them. So we never find this relationship.

Consider what would happen if I did this with my wife. Suppose I arrived home after some days of work away, and on my way I met a 'friend' who said, 'Hey, Rog, you've been away for some time, haven't you? Well, a lot of funny people have been going in and out of your house. I don't know who your wife has around there when you're not at home!'

As I listen to what he says I could do one of two things: I could either begin to doubt my wife's integrity, or I could be sensible and say to myself, 'Well, everything I know about my wife is trustworthy. She gives herself sacrificially for the children and me. She is always, to my knowledge, very loving and faithful . . . that is what I know about her. So I'm going to major on that.' In that case I would brush off the doubt that might have been planted in my mind and would go into my home saying, 'How've you been getting on while I've been away, my darling? Has everything has gone well?' And straight away we have set up a loving, trusting relationship again. But suppose I went in saying, 'Now what's all this I've been hearing about you?' then I am unlikely to be able to build a relationship with her.

Similarly I cannot encounter and begin a relationship with God unless I use the little bit of faith I have already to build on. I have to major on the fact that there is enough evidence to demonstrate that God is more likely to be there than he is not; and that there is sufficient indication to suggest that the claims of Jesus Christ are reasonable.

If I thus begin to move in faith, in prayer, in that direction, and give myself to God, trusting what I know, then doubts will gradually be replaced by knowledge, and I will have a faith that gets bigger and bigger. To get off the ground in trusting God you have to take that small bit of knowledge of him and use it; so your faith will grow every day, and you will get stronger and stronger in the reality of the God who is getting involved with you. Facts are to be used in faith when building a relationship. All stable relationships require faith built on facts, and sensible people do not concentrate on doubtful speculations.

A WHOLE NEW BALL GAME

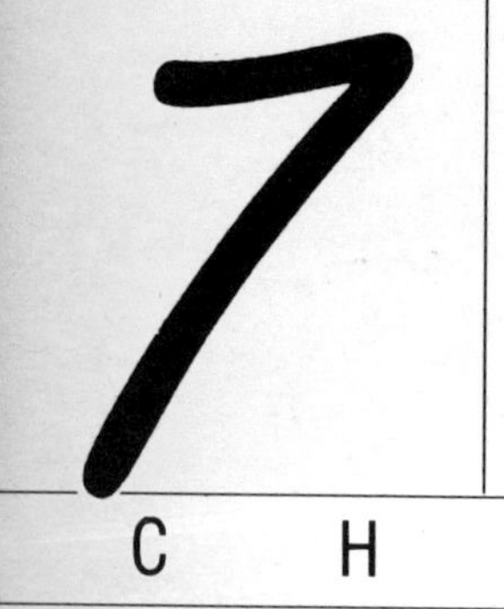

C H A P T E R

When we begin to get involved with God and receive from him forgiveness and new life, three things, amongst others, begin to take place – three things that will drive us out into the world with a wholly different attitude.

"The life in a frog's egg aims at producing a frog."

New life

The first thing that happens is that *we find that God's life in us*, through that encounter with Jesus Christ, brings us to a *purpose*. It is not always a purpose that we can spell out exactly at the very beginning of our Christian experience, but like all life, we know it has a direction. The life in a frog's egg aims at producing a frog. Even though the jelly-enveloped egg initially releases a tadpole, because of the genetic information in each cell it will fulfil its destiny and become a frog. The life that was in the embryo in your mother's womb has now moved out into what we see in you today. There is a direction and a purpose in life. And God's life has a purpose. We sense that purpose even though we, as Christians, may not be able to define fully where it is going.

". . . we should become supersonic angels . . ."

I hinted at what this purpose is at the beginning of the last chapter. It is to make us perfect, or perhaps more fully, it is to make us sons and daughters of God, patterned after his own Son. God did not choose that we should become supersonic angels; nor, from the beginning of time, did he choose that we should become high-powered psychedelic beasts.

God's purpose, from the foundation of the world, is that we should take on the character, life, wisdom, purpose, communion, business and family life of God himself, by becoming daughters and sons of God. This will involve us in being 'women and men for others', as Christ was *par excellence*, and serving God's interests by serving our fellow men and women as Christ did, being called a servant and saying himself that he came to serve and not to be served.

The adventure begins. When I become a Christian and receive that life of God, I begin to find God's purpose pulsating through my being to make me like his Son; to make me love like his son, bear suffering as his Son, to live sacrificially like his Son, to carry the mercy of God to others as his Son carries it . . . and so on. Even more, a son or daughter can look into his or her father's face and say 'Father', and get to know him. That is the over-all purpose which God brings into our experience when we become Christians.

Of course, this major eternal purpose will have its reflection in some subsidiary purposes – micro-affairs connected with this temporal life. One Christian is going to have an adventure with God in the academic world; another in the engineering department; another in agriculture, in music, or in the home, or entertainment, or business: there are a thousand and one things in which to be involved with the life of God; situations in which God is wanting to involve himself and get working with us.

"We have a new power."

I don't know what your adventure will be. God has different ones for different people, in different places and at different times. Each is the particular exploit best suited to the person you are, the work he wants to do with you, and the people he wants to involve you with. To be in a life with God is absolutely unlimited in its possibilities. We must expose ourselves and be available for that encounter, so that he may take over and start to share eternal life with us.

New power

The second great thing that happens is that *we discover a new power*. All of us at times must have known: 'I cannot do the good I want, but the evil I do not want is what I do.' This is our bankruptcy. This is the failure of our poverty. It comes partly from the kick-back of the environment into which we have been pitched, partly from the heredity that we have gained from the human race. The result is, 'I cannot do the good I want, but the evil I do not want is what I do.'

(Romans 7:19)

The eternal life of God brings a power to work within us so that step by step, assuredly and significantly, we begin to embrace our failure and overcome it. We have a new power.

". . . involved in occult practices . . ."

A broken relationship. I remember some years ago a young man phoned me. I was reluctant to talk with him because I knew all about his problem and my previous attempts to advise him had been fruitless. He had been unfaithful to his wife many times and seemed incapable of seeing how deeply he was hurting her. Now finally he was faced with the prospect of divorce, which he did not really want.

His latest 'affair' was with a girl involved in occult practices and she seemed to have such a hold on him that he was unable to end the relationship. Now he was desperate. So he drove the few miles to my house and rang the doorbell.

Just then, by a remarkable coincidence, his wife walked up the path. She had felt equally desperate and had come to see if my wife could help her. She had come by train, he by car, and they had quite unexpectedly met on the doorstep! We hastily parted them.

"Are you prepared to talk . . . about it?"

I began to talk to the man. His whole attitude was selfish and egocentric; he was concerned with what he was going to lose, how he was suffering, what it meant to him, with no thought of what he was doing to his wife. After a couple of hours of this I asked him, 'Are you prepared to talk to God about it?' To my surprise he answered, 'Yes, I will.' And he started to pray.

When you pray in this kind of situation, you realize it is useless to try to 'con' God. You have to be honest and real. I had read him verses from the New Testament that urge 'Husbands, love your wives' – with no ifs or buts!

(Ephesians 5:28)

So he confessed honestly, 'God, I have never loved my wife. Please forgive me. And will you help me?' That was the most sincere thing he had said all evening! We both prayed on our knees, then sat down again. Suddenly God's power began to come upon him and he started to shake, then to cry. To see a strong man cry is always rather overwhelming, so I got him on his knees again and he wept as he poured out his heart to God and found forgiveness of sins.

". . . those were his exact words."

At last we sat back again in our chairs and he said to me, 'Roger, I've never felt so clean in all my life.' Then he added, 'You know, I saw the Lord.' 'What do you mean, you saw the Lord?' 'Well,' he said, 'I saw him high and lifted up. I didn't see his face or anything but I just knew that he was lifted up above all this situation.' Now those were his exact words.

At this point I thought it was about time to bring in his wife. My wife and I left them, since there was a touching reconciliation scene between the two. I asked my wife, 'How did you get on with her?' She replied,

'Well, I felt she was having the rough side of the situation, so I was praying that God would give me something to help her. And he gave me Isaiah chapter 6. So I read from the sixth chapter of Isaiah and said to her, "We must pray for your husband that he *sees the Lord*, because he does not feel his sin." '

I was amazed and said to my wife, 'Do you know what he has just said to me?' and I told her. Now this is how Isaiah chapter 6 reads:

'In the year that King Uzziah died I saw the Lord . . . high and lifted up; and his train filled the temple . . . and the house was filled with smoke (speaking of the mysterious presence of God). The doorposts shook at his presence and the seraphim cried, 'Holy, holy, holy is the Lord of hosts; the whole earth is full of his glory.' Isaiah then cried out and said, 'I am a man of unclean lips, and I dwell in the midst of a people of unclean lips; for my eyes have seen the King, the Lord of hosts!' And a coal was taken from the altar (a picture of the place of sacrifice where Christ, the great sacrifice of God himself was offered up for the world) and it was laid on Isaiah's lips and his sin was purged.

That was Isaiah's experience thousands of years ago, and that night it had been the experience of this young man. 'I have never felt so clean in all my life,' he had said. 'I saw the Lord high and lifted up above all this situation.'

Six months later I took him with me to a meeting some miles away. On the way home, he said, 'Oh Rog, can't you put your foot down on that accelerator? This is the longest I have been away from my wife since we came to your house that night, and I'm really missing her. You know, I was a fool to look at any other woman. My wife has been such a help to me. You'd never believe what a wonderful life we have together now as we help each other in knowing God!' He had found a *power* in God to make a new man of himself. Hardly surprising that he makes his first aim now the business of Jesus Christ.

'You'd never believe . . .''

New love

Thirdly, *there is a passion which eternal life brings* when we welcome Christ into our lives, a passion for God which overspills in love for others. I remember taking some meetings in a university where there was someone who went to his room after one of the meetings and, desiring to do God's will, simply asked Jesus Christ to come and take over his life. The following weekend we went to his home in an area where there lived many Asian immigrants. He had been brought up to hate immigrants. His father's job depended on there not being too many immigrants, or so he was led to believe.

As he walked down the street that Saturday morning, he saw an Asian man coming along on the other side of the road. Suddenly he was surprised at himself, he was aware that something had changed in him. The man who, a few days before, had spoken words to the effect, 'All right, God, I want to start going your way, will you get involved with me?' found that he was looking at that Pakistani man with a love which he had not known before. He had a new outlook which later on took him into the immigrant scene with a desire to share Jesus Christ, and to work for those who have come as strangers to this country and are seeking to find a proper place in it.

The love of God overspills when we let it into our lives. It gives us the motivation, not for far-distant scenes about which we can only dream, but for the immediate scene and wherever God will ultimately place us in this world, to meet the real needs of men and women – to be loved, and to discover reality, and to be involved in God's movement – making *real* people for his kingdom.

Close encounter

But this will happen only when we come to God and admit that, though we may like to pretend to be 'beautiful people', our lives are really rather ugly. And you and I find it so hard to come and stand before God and say, 'I need you. I am bankrupt, but I want this life that you offer.' We find it so hard to repent and say, 'I'm sorry.'

This is the problem. Only good people have the humility to say they are sorry and repent, but it is only bad people that need to repent. It is so humbling to say you are sorry, that you were wrong, and that you need help. It takes more humility than most of us have.

Perhaps that is one of the many things that Jesus Christ did for us when he died on the cross. Because he was a good person and had nothing to repent of, he was able to go through a repentance for us, to experience the humiliation of being sorry and repenting,

". . . something had changed . . ."

of hanging his head in shame, and saying, 'My God, my God, why . . . ?' As a good person, he could do it; he could humble himself to that degree, so that when we come fumblingly to God, trying to do it, he is there to help us.

It's just like a child trying to write letters. He makes a scrawl, until Father puts his hand over the child's hand and, because he has the ability, does it perfectly for and with the child.

Perhaps you are saying you do not feel sorry enough; perhaps you don't feel bad enough. Maybe you never will, but you still have to repent. If you come just as you are, Jesus Christ will help you because he knows exactly what you are going to go through and what he has been through, and he puts his hand over yours and helps you to say, 'I'm sorry. I'm only fit for the crucifixion that Jesus had, only fit to be written off as waste. I certainly have not got in me the ability to take up my cross daily and follow him, the lifestyle that he calls me to. But I believe that if he comes with me I will have a new life and a new power. Please come into my life, Lord Jesus Christ, and start this eternal life of God in me.'

"It takes more humility than most of us have."

Then you have started on the process which God intends for every woman and man – life with a purpose, with a new power and with a love for God. It is possible really to love God! And as you begin to love him you will find that beauty, that love in you overspilling to other people.

IN THE END . . . GOD

In the face of some pretty depressing evidence to the contrary, people down the ages have often believed in a hope and a dream, a future utopia or a golden age of peace and prosperity. Even though in our own century, now drawing to a close, numerous examples of inhumanity, war upon war, famine and environmental peril all signal that there is no hope. We only have to look to the environmental scientists and population statisticians to see how rapidly our own self-destruction is approaching us. Yet still the hope burns on. For Christians, who believe that in the beginning is God, the end will not come with the human race on its own with its great kingdom but with God himself. God will continue to intervene and the hope will be realized, not in our way, but in God's way and in God's world.

Despite the bleak prediction that the end of the human race is a real possibility, Christians maintain their hope for the return of Jesus with good reason. The remarkable fulfilment of the Bible's historical prophecies of the coming of Jesus encourages us to believe him when he says 'I will come again and take you to myself' and 'My kingdom will come . . . pray for it.' (Try reading Psalm 22; Isaiah 7:14; Isaiah 53 and Micah 5:2.) Indeed, this hope is for 'a new heaven and a new earth' as the Bible describes it.

In view of the accuracies of the prophecies about Jesus, we ought to listen to what he tells us will happen when his new age is ushered in in due time. We will each receive a verdict based on whether our lives have flowed in the stream of truth, or in the stream of the lie. Did we play at being gods and set ourselves up in our own kingdom, or have we acknowledged the God and Creator of all as central, even finding his son, the Lord Jesus Christ, as the truth? It will be a judgment on the real

". . . and the truth will set you free."

(John 8:32)

beauty which exists in our inner lives, when they are stripped of our unfortunately inherited dispositions. We will stand before God as naked spirits who have chosen either love or hate, pride or humility, bitterness or forgiveness, oppression or mercy. The inner choice of our spirits will be exposed before the Almighty God.

If truth 'sets man free' then untruth would bring us into bondage and must be destroyed. We will stand before God, the small and the great, and the books of our lives will be opened. What we are will be there, and what we are includes what we have done – we cannot change that. Each person will be judged as to whether he or she is in the kingdom of our God and of his Christ.

Now the Bible tells us that the wages of sin, that is its consequences, are death. But those who accept God's judgment on us now and simply plead 'guilty' (not blaming society, heredity, family or environment) will find that God meets us at the place where the sentence was carried out; Calvary, where Jesus died for us. Then we shall not face the penalty for our sin but pass from death to life. We can be part of God's kingdom by accepting his truth now. '. . . You will know the truth,' says Jesus, 'and the truth will set you free.'